DRUG REGULATION
AND INNOVATION

Evaluative Studies

This series of studies seeks to bring about greater understanding and promote continuing review of the activities and functions of the federal government. Each study focuses on a specific program, evaluating its cost and efficiency, the extent to which it achieves its objectives, and the major alternative means—public and private—for reaching those objectives. Yale Brozen, professor of economics at the University of Chicago and an adjunct scholar of the American Enterprise Institute for Public Policy Research, is the director of the program.

DRUG REGULATION AND INNOVATION

Empirical evidence and policy options

Henry G. Grabowski

American Enterprise Institute for Public Policy Research
Washington, D.C.

This study is one of a series published by the American Enterprise Institute as part of the research program of AEI's Center for Health Policy Research. A distinguished advisory committee, whose members are listed below, helps guide this program.

ISBN 0-8447-3217-6

Evaluative Studies 28, September 1976

Library of Congress Catalog Card No. 76-25709

Printed in the United States of America

CONTENTS

FOREWORD

The U.S. comparative advantage in international trade lies in its research intensive industries.[1] Their products have played an increasing role in the growth of exports and have contributed to the strength of the dollar. One leader in this group has been the pharmaceutical industry. Exports of medicinal and pharmaceutical products nearly tripled their share of U.S. merchandise exports from the prewar period to the 1950s [2] with the earnings from foreign operations of U.S. pharmaceutical companies showing even more dramatic growth.[3] But Professor Grabowski finds that changes now under way show slipping U.S. leadership in pharmaceutical research and production. Continuation of the new trend

---

[1] D. B. Keesing, "The Impact of Research and Development on U.S. Trade," *Journal of Political Economy,* vol. 75, no. 1 (February 1967), pp. 38-48; W. Gruber, D. Mehta and R. Vernon, "The R & D Factor in International Trade and International Investment of U.S. Industries," in ibid., pp. 20-37.

[2] Computed from data in various issues of *Statistical Abstract of the United States.*

[3] The FDA has forced U.S. firms to manufacture more and more abroad in recent years because of increasing delays in approval of New Drug Applications (NDAs). "Regulations prohibit drugs from being exported without an approved NDA. With the greatly increased time required to attain NDA approval . . . in 1975 twelve new chemical NDAs were approved with an average of over eight years from IND filing to NDA approval . . . indeed with the possibility that it might never be approved here—there is more and more of a pattern for U.S. firms to introduce a new drug in a number of foreign countries before attempting to market it in the United States. Being unable to export from the United States, these firms must establish production facilities abroad. . . ." *New Drugs: Pending Legislation* (Washington, D.C.: American Enterprise Institute for Public Policy Research, 1976), p. 49. See also comments by Halberstam and Lasagna, *Reforming Federal Drug Regulation* (Washington, D.C.: American Enterprise Institute, 1976), pp. 2-3.

will further erode the role of the dollar as an international currency and as a pillar of U.S. prestige.

An indication of the change is the decline in discovery and development of new chemical entities by U.S. firms—an initial decline from more than one-third of worldwide introductions in the year before the 1962 amendments to the Food, Drug, and Cosmetic Act to less than one-quarter of the total in 1963 (see Table 5), and unfortunately, as Professor Grabowski shows, a continued erosion of U.S. leadership thereafter. We have reached the point where innovations based on discoveries by U.S. firms and institutions constitute less than one-sixth of worldwide introductions of new chemical entities (see Table 5), and exports of pharmaceuticals as a share of U.S. exports have declined by one-third since the 1950s.

While declining U.S. leadership in pharmaceutical innovation may erode our international economic position, it would not necessarily cause a loss of benefit to the sick in the United States if drugs developed abroad were made available here. Many are, but a growing proportion is not. While worldwide introductions of new chemical entities declined by 28 percent from 1961 to 1973 (see Table 5), those allowed on the U.S. market declined by 53 percent (see Table 1). Some have been drugs of choice in other countries, while they were not available on the U.S. market. Anomalous situations develop where U.S. doctors send patients abroad for treatment in order to use a drug not available here.[4]

One of the bitter ironies of this situation is that the 1962 amendments were spurred by an alarm over the *safety* of new drugs—by the fears created by the thalidomide incident. The irony lies in the fact that the 1962 amendments are keeping off the market new drugs that are safer than the drugs they would replace. Professor William Wardell's study of the lags in the introduction of new drugs in the United States cites, as one example, the five-year delay in the appearance on the U.S. market of a benzodiazepine hypnotic. If it had been available in the United States as it was in Great Britain during those five years, Professor Wardell estimates that 1,200 lives would have been saved.[5]

---

[4] For accounts of two such examples, see Richard R. Leger, "Viral Venereal Disease Is Highly Contagious and Doesn't Go Away," *Wall Street Journal*, April 19, 1974, and comments by M. Halberstam and L. Lasagna, *Reforming Federal Drug Regulation*, pp. 2-3.

[5] William M. Wardell, "Therapeutic Implications of the Drug Lag," *Clinical Pharmacology and Therapeutics*, vol. 15, no. 1 (January 1974), p. 83. See also

An additional source of irony is the fact that a major reason for the delays and the decline in the rate of introduction of new drugs is that the FDA is required by the 1962 amendments to pass on the effectiveness of new drugs. It already had the duty prior to 1962 to pass on the safety of new drugs before they could be marketed, a requirement that was not changed by the 1962 amendments. The 1962 congressional response to the thalidomide incident was largely a *non sequitur.*[6]

The 1962 amendments to the Food, Drug, and Cosmetic Act have caused more than a "drug lag" in the United States. There has also been a decline in drug innovation. The FDA and others have argued that the U.S. decline is simply the result of a depletion of research opportunities. But the fact that the drop in the U.S. innovation rate has been much sharper than the drop in the innovation rate in the rest of the world—especially in the face of increasingly strict regulation abroad—contradicts the FDA position. Before 1962 the rate of new chemical introductions in the United States was a little less than one-half the worldwide rate. In the decade following, the U.S. rate dropped to little more than one-fifth the worldwide rate (see Tables 1 and 5). If it could be shown that the drop was the result of unimportant, ineffective, or dangerous drugs being kept off the U.S. market, we could rest content. But Professor Grabowski's comparison of U.S. and British experience contradicts this hypothesis.

The U.S. decline from one-half to one-fifth the worldwide rate of innovation is a decrease in a proportion of decreased innovation. Professor Grabowski points out that the decreasing worldwide rate of innovation is likewise (at least to some extent, if not entirely) a consequence of the 1962 amendments. Requirements for permission to market in the United States affect foreign as well as U.S. firms. Since the U.S. market is a major portion of the worldwide market, a doubling of the cost of obtaining clear-

---

the comments by Bureau of Drugs (FDA) director, Dr. Richard Crout, as quoted in Rita Ricardo Campbell, *Drug Lag* (Stanford, Calif.: Hoover Institution Press, 1976), p. 34.
[6] The 1962 amendments did add a requirement that no investigation of toxicity and therapeutic effects in human beings could begin until thirty days after filing a new-drug investigational plan (IND) giving the results of animal tests and detailing proposed research protocols for human tests. The FDA was also given the power to halt new-drug investigations if it felt that any data supplied at that point or later threatened the safety of human volunteers. In view of prior experience, however, this new power was not required to improve safety. E. A. Carr, discussion in "Clinical Pharmacology and the Human Volunteer," *Clinical Pharmacology and Therapeutics,* vol. 13, no. 5, Part II (1972), pp. 790-795.

ance for U.S. marketing [7] reduces the return to investment in research and development, to foreign as well as domestic firms, and therefore reduces the number of projects undertaken and innovations produced in spite of an increase in the resources devoted to research and development. All the additional resources and more have been diverted to meeting the new requirements.

To reduce the drug lag and raise the rate of innovation, a number of regulatory reforms have been suggested. Several bills have been introduced in Congress with this objective.[8] Professor Grabowski examines some of the proposed reforms, particularly those designed to reduce the asymmetry in incentives motivating FDA personnel. Any actual or possible harm resulting from permitting new drugs to be marketed produces strong censure of FDA personnel but little reward or praise is given for quickly clearing those drugs with large benefits for the sick.[9] Iatrogenic effects are emblazoned in headlines while the life that is not saved by the drug that has not been invented—or, if invented, remains uncleared—is little noted.

Surprisingly, Professor Grabowski favors a diffusion of responsibility for the clearance of a drug—I say "surprisingly"

---

[7] Professor David Schwartzman, in *The Expected Return from Pharmaceutical Research* (Washington, D.C.: American Enterprise Institute, 1975), estimates that the average research and development cost of a new chemical entity as of 1973 amounted to $24.4 million (p. 28) exclusive of the cost of capital invested in research and development. As of 1960, he estimates research and development costs per new chemical entity of $1.3 million (p. 42). This eighteen-fold increase in costs would have been only a nine-fold increase according to independent estimates by Professor Sam Peltzman (*Regulation of Pharmaceutical Innovation* [Washington, D.C.: American Enterprise Institute, 1974], p. 112), and Professor Martin Baily ("Research and Development Cost and Returns: The U.S. Pharmaceutical Industry," *Journal of Political Economy,* vol. 60, no. 1 [January/February 1972], p. 78) if the 1962 amendments had not been passed. The nine-fold increase was expected to occur because of the increasing amount of testing for safety as new procedures were developed enabling the performance of new tests and because of inflation. An indirect confirmation of the doubling of research and development costs caused by the 1962 amendments is provided by Britain's National Economic Development Office, *Focus on Pharmaceuticals* (London: Her Majesty's Stationery Office, 1972), which pointed out that "the UK's innovative efficiency was between 2 and 2½ times that of the U.S." (p. x).

[8] Symms Bill—H.R. 14426; Kennedy-Javits Bill—S. 2697; Rogers et al. Bill—H.R. 14289; all 94th Congress.

[9] This is, in part, a consequence to be expected from the bias in the assembly of data concerning the effects of a drug released for general use. Professors Lasagna and Wardell point out that "A situation has arisen in which we now have methodology available which, while defective, is being used to estimate the total harm of drugs to the community; but we have no comparable methodology available for measuring the total benefit of drugs to the community." (*Regulation and Drug Development,* p. 95).

because one of the usual hallmarks of an effective administrative structure is the focusing of responsibility. In the case of FDA review officers, however, the risk from releasing any drug is large and the benefit small even though the risks to patients may be small and the benefits large. It is to meet the problems created by the perverse relationship of the risk-benefit ratio for FDA officers to the risk-benefit ratio for patients that moves Professor Grabowski to this unusual position.

One method of diffusing responsibility suggested by Professor Grabowski is the use of a committee of "professional advisers whose careers and reputation are firmly established outside the regulatory process." [10] This suggestion is drawn from the experience of the British regulatory system, which seems to have suffered fewer and shorter delays in allowing drugs to come to market than those caused by dilatory, supercautious FDA reviewing officers.

The FDA, under the leadership of Commissioner Alexander Schmidt and Bureau of Drugs Director Richard Crout, has moved, in the last few years, toward the approach suggested here by Professor Grabowski. It has increasingly used committees of well-known experts to appraise pharmacological data, and it has moved responsibility for questioning sponsors of new drugs and for approving or disapproving the marketing of new drugs from reviewing officers as individuals to supervisors acting for the agency. [11] The result in at least some instances has been a quickening of the decision process and a decrease in the number of roadblocks created by idiosyncratic behavior.[12]

Another suggestion from Professor Grabowski, which he believes "offers a number of potential advantages over the current system," is "a system of gradual monitored release of new drugs." [13] He is much more sanguine than I am about this approach. If it takes the form of the "Phase D" activity proposed in the Kennedy-Javits Bill,[14] it will simply become another "cop-out"

---

[10] See p. 78 below.

[11] There has been resentment by reviewing officers of the decline in their power, and some disgruntled officers have made spectacular, but unsubstantiated, charges against the agency before congressional committees.

[12] W. M. Wardell, "Developments in the Introduction of New Drugs in the United States and Britain, 1971-74," in Robert B. Helms, ed., Drug Development and Marketing (Washington, D.C.: American Enterprise Institute for Public Policy Research, 1975), pp. 165-181.

[13] See p. 79 below.

[14] See New Drugs: Pending Legislation, pp. 27-32, for an analysis of the proposal.

for FDA reviewers, by which they can further delay the release of drugs for general use, further reduce the incentives for the research and development investment required to produce pharmaceutical innovations, and further erode U.S. leadership in pharmaceutical innovation and production. Perhaps some of these potential effects can be ameliorated by putting an absolute one-year time limit on Phase D, but this new roadblock is likely to be as counterproductive as those added by the 1962 amendments.

Perhaps the perversity of FDA reviewing officers stems fundamentally from the role in which they have been cast. Legislation has cast those who would market the medicines we need in the role of malefactors intent on robbing the public by selling ineffective drugs—malefactors quite as willing as burglars with guns to damage those from whom they seek to extract funds. Reviewing officers, then, think of themselves as policemen stopping burglars from plying their trade. They cast themselves in the role of stopping new drugs from reaching the market where they would defraud and damage unsuspecting customers.

What neither Congress nor FDA officers recognize is that the drugs that are most profitable for manufacturers are those that are the safest and most effective. Drugs that are found to be too toxic and that must be recalled are extremely costly (in damage payments, for example) to marketers, who therefore have strong incentives to keep them off the market. A bad batch of polio vaccine, for example, cost Cutter Laboratories $3 million in settling damage claims, and they were not even found criminally negligent, while A. H. Robins Co. has already paid out $3 million in damage settlements on the Dalkon Shield intrauterine device, with many more claims pending.[15] All drugs that reach the market today must meet FDA proof of efficacy, but those without real advantages over existing ones are also costly. They do not sell well and fail to return the investment in their development and promotion.[16] It is simply not profitable to invest in developing and marketing unsafe or ineffective pharmaceuticals (or even "me too" products with no greater efficacy than those currently available) since it is safe effective drugs that are the most profitable.[17] It is

[15] N. Nathanson and A. D. Langmuir, "The Cutter Incident. Poliomyelitis Following Formaldehyde Inactivated Polio Virus Vaccine in the United States during the Spring of 1955," *American Journal of Hygiene,* vol. 78 (July 1963), p. 24, and *Wall Street Journal,* August 19, 1976, p. 17.

[16] Peltzman, *Regulation of Pharmaceutical Innovation,* p. 45.

[17] An example illustrating this observation is provided by SKF experience. "In 1936 the younger managers . . . convinced Mr. Kline that the firm was

not Marshal Petains that are needed at the FDA. We would be better served by officers who are cast in the role of county agricultural agents than by those who cry, "They shall not pass." Pharmaceutical firms are not burglars taking from the public: they are much more like farmers making their profits by feeding the public.

The reforms needed in drug legislation and at the FDA are, therefore, those that will change the role of the FDA reviewing officer from that of a policeman, stopping drugs from reaching the market, to that of a county agricultural agent, assisting firms to bring safe, effective aids to good health to the market as quickly as possible. A small step in this direction would be to eliminate the FDA's power to require substantial evidence of effectiveness. This, at least, has the virtue of partially removing one of the roadblocks that now delay the availability of drugs that would widen the array of choice for the treatment of illness.[18] Furthermore, it has been demonstrated that the incidence of ineffectiveness among new drugs was not lessened by the requirement imposed in 1962. The requirement was redundant. As Professor Peltzman has shown, "The penalties imposed by the marketplace on sellers

---

. . . losing money on the hundreds of USP and NF items it made and that the profit was generated by three specialty products. . . . Why? Because each . . . promotional dollar generated more sales and profits if the product had distinctive superiority and advantages for the physician." Harold A. Clymer, "The Economic and Regulatory Climate: U.S. and Overseas Trends," in Helms, Drug Development and Marketing, p. 139.

[18] The widened array of choice is important in the treatment of patients even if the new drugs are no more effective than those already available. Professor Wardell has pointed out that "Failure to show a difference in efficacy between a new drug and an older one should not be taken to mean that the new drug cannot be a worthwhile advance. . . . First, each drug's efficacy may be exerted on a different segment of the population; if both drugs were available, the proportion of patients treatable might be much higher than if either drug were available alone. By the same argument, a drug that is 'on average' less effective and more toxic than existing therapy may still be highly desirable for some segments of the population. Our current simplistic statistical concepts of efficacy and safety usually fail to take this into account. Second, it is common to find that the spectrum of side effects differs for each drug, or that the pharmacokinetics are different enough to confer different dosage regimens upon each drug. Third, in the actual treatment of many types of conditions, a patient should receive several drugs in turn on a trial-and-error basis until the one that is best for his needs is determined empirically. These realities of therapeutics for individual patients are generally ignored in the current requirements for evidence of drug efficacy. All these factors can be crucial for tailoring therapy to an individual patient to achieve maximal efficacy, safety, comfort, convenience, and compliance with the therapeutic regimen. To achieve these goals it is desirable to have a number of alternative therapies from which to choose." Wardell, "Therapeutic Implications of the Drug Lag," p. 76.

of ineffective drugs before 1962 seem to have been sufficient to have left little room for improvement by a regulatory agency." [19]

We have received little benefit from the 1962 amendment, and we are paying large penalties. The sick are being deprived of effective treatment for some of their ailments. Drugs, some of which are drugs of choice, are available abroad but not here. The rate of pharmaceutical innovation has been depressed, further depriving those in need of effective treatment. The international position of the U.S. pharmaceutical industry has suffered a setback that is apparently growing more severe. Our share of innovations is declining and pharmaceutical research is shifting to overseas locations.[20] This is having undesirable effects on the value of the dollar and on U.S. prestige, and a secondary impact (which has not yet been measured) is likely to be shown in depressed support for academic pharmacology and less rapid advance in basic knowledge. These are all "benefits" of the 1962 amendments which I, for one, am quite willing to do without.

Yale Brozen

Graduate School of Business
University of Chicago

---

[19] Peltzman, *Regulation of Pharmaceutical Innovation,* p. 45 (italics in original not reproduced here).

[20] Clymer, "Economic and Regulatory Climate," pp. 142-154.

PREFACE

This study is an outgrowth of a paper I was asked to prepare for a government agency with policy interest and responsibilities in the area of regulation and innovation. My assigned task was to review what was known about the impacts of regulation on pharmaceutical innovation and to evaluate various policy options for improving regulatory performance. About a decade earlier, I had undertaken a study of what determined innovation in the pharmaceutical industry. My new assignment afforded me an opportunity to "catch up" with recent developments.

As I began sifting through different sources of data, through academic papers, and through congressional testimony on the industry, I became increasingly impressed with the degree to which innovational activity in the drug industry had changed since the period covered by my earlier study (the late 1950s and early 1960s). The earlier period, of course, predated the 1962 amendments to the Food, Drug, and Cosmetic Act and various other developments. It has been characterized by some as the golden period of pharmaceutical innovation and discovery in the United States. A number of adverse developments have taken place in subsequent years, including a rate of new product introductions which now is on average about one-fourth the rate in the earlier period.

This paper presents my analysis and interpretation of the evidence relating the change in the rate of innovation to regulation and to other factors. Since we are far from fully defining the causes of the change, I have tried to focus attention throughout the study on areas for further research in the hope that it will stimulate additional analysis by other researchers. Over the two or so years that have elapsed since I first began work on this project, I myself have become involved in research on this subject and the results from some recently completed papers are also summarized here.

While this study focuses on developments in the pharmaceutical industry, I believe the findings will have increasing importance and applicability over time to other sectors. This is because actual and potential regulation of product quality standards has increased dramatically in recent years. For example, Congress has created the Consumer Product Safety Commission which is empowered to establish mandatory standards and regulate labeling for any class of products which this agency finds to be unsafe. In addition, other product classes are now being considered for pre-market clearance procedures similar to that which has existed in drugs. The drug industry with its longer track record of product quality regulation offers one of the few empirical bases for assessing the benefits and costs of these proposed new fields of regulation.

The final chapter of the study outlines a set of possible policy options for improving regulatory incentives with respect to innovation. This material also should be of interest to readers interested in general aspects of regulation as well as those directly concerned with product quality regulation of ethical drugs.

I am grateful to a number of individuals who provided helpful comments to me as this manuscript evolved. I owe a special debt to John Vernon who commented extensively on the first draft and subsequently collaborated on two research studies that are discussed in the text. I also wish to thank several others who read later drafts and made several helpful suggestions for improving the manuscript. They are Yale Brozen, Carol Chapman, Harold Clymer, Dianne Davenny, Louis Lasagna, Robert Helms, Lacy Thomas, and William Wardell.

CHAPTER I

INTRODUCTION AND OVERVIEW OF ISSUES IN ETHICAL DRUG REGULATION

Regulations governing the introduction of new drugs into the United States are intended to ensure that all drugs introduced be safe and effective. Implementation of the law is in the hands of a regulatory body, the Food and Drug Administration (FDA), which has considerable discretion over the evaluation and approval process. FDA officials have characterized the decision-making process as one in which all of the evidence on a drug's safety and efficacy is evaluated within a benefit/risk framework.[1] The evaluation forms the basis for a drug's approval or disapproval.

Market Failure as a Rationale for Drug Regulation

Presumably, the rationale for giving a regulatory agent the power to make a collective decision for society as a whole is to correct what economists label as a "market failure." In this instance, the failure postulated is that the forces of the free market would lead to the consumption of many drugs possessing excessive risks in relation to their benefits. The hypothesized source of this market failure is a lack of information on the part of drug consumers—in other words, patients and prescribing doctors—and a lack of incentives for pharmaceutical firms to provide sufficient information.

In the early stages of development, attempts to determine a drug's total benefits and total risks are characterized by con-

---

[1] See, for example, the testimony of Henry Simmons before the U.S. Congress, Senate, Select Committee on Small Business, *Competitive Problems in the Drug Industry,* Part 23, 92d Congress, February 1972 (Washington, D.C.: U.S. Government Printing Office, 1972).

siderable uncertainty. The degree of uncertainty can be reduced by various kinds of tests on animals and humans. The trade-offs in this information-generating process are themselves subject to uncertainty. The current delegation of decision-making power to a centralized regulatory agent is based on the notion that profit incentives and market competition are insufficient to generate a socially optimal level of information or to produce a socially desirable decision by business firms, given a particular level of knowledge about a drug's potential benefits and risks.

The incentives of the marketplace, under this condition of uncertainty, are therefore seen as leading to errors and abuses of considerable consequence. Firms, in order to gain competitive advantage over rivals or simply to avoid high costs, may devote inadequate time and resources to pre-market testing. In addition, firms are thought to have an incentive to overstate good points and understate negative ones in promoting new drugs and disseminating information through labeling and advertising. The consequences of these actions, even if subject to self-correction through experience over the long run, are viewed as entailing unacceptable social costs.

This approximately summarizes the case for delegating decision-making power in drugs to a regulatory body. Of course it is not clear how, in the face of the same uncertainty that affects private endeavors, a public agency can rationally determine the optimal level of resources to be devoted to obtaining information on a drug's safety and efficacy before the drug is generally released. The enactment of the Food, Drug, and Cosmetic Act of 1938 and the Kefauver-Harris Amendments of 1962 both followed highly publicized drug disasters.[2] The decision-making power to determine the optimal level of information was concentrated in a regulatory body, the FDA. Apparently, little thought was given to the problems that this in turn might present or to the possibility that such an agency itself might produce errors, albeit of a different nature from any errors produced by the forces of the marketplace.

Advocates of a market-oriented system of drug innovation emphasize the fact that the regulatory process is not costless to

---

[2] The first law regulating drugs was the Food and Drug Act of 1906 which prohibited adulteration and mislabeling of food and drugs sold in interstate commerce. Implementation of this law was plagued by a number of problems and the law proved generally ineffective. For an historical discussion, see Clair Wilcox, *Public Policies Toward Business,* 3rd edition (Homewood, Illinois: Richard D. Irwin, 1966).

consumers. In particular they argue that any benefits it conveys in the increased probability of safety and efficacy for approved drugs must be weighed against the time delays and reduced levels of innovation resulting from the regulatory process. Even if one assumes a highly efficient and competent regulatory body, there would necessarily be a trade-off between the stringency of regulatory standards and the level of drug innovation—that is, as regulatory standards become more demanding, more resources must be devoted to pre-market testing and development cost and time will therefore increase. As a consequence, some drugs of a beneficial character will no longer be profitable to develop. In addition, consumers will generally have to wait longer to receive the benefits of those drugs that are developed and marketed.

Furthermore, critics of the FDA regulatory process emphasize the fact that the incentives operating in a regulatory body like the FDA will make that body relatively insensitive to the costs of time delays and lessened innovations.[3] Rather, such a regulatory body will tend to err on the side of excessive caution and safety, inasmuch as the body stands to pay a heavy penalty if it approves a drug with serious unforeseen adverse effects. On the other hand, the social costs of time delays and lessened innovation are not only less visible but are borne entirely by parties other than the FDA officials.

In sum, regulation generally entails both costs and benefits. One therefore cannot justify regulation solely by enumerating the failures of the market. The benefits and costs of regulation must be compared to the benefits and costs of the "market failure" situation the regulation is designed to correct. Under a proper system of accounting, consumer welfare might be reduced on balance by regulation from its state in a more market-oriented situation.

Of course, society is not restricted to a choice between an entirely market-oriented system on the one hand and an entirely centralized system of regulatory controls on the other. A whole spectrum of policy options exists between these extremes. Given the uncertainties described above, however, one cannot know a priori what policy measures will yield the best outcome from

---

[3] See, for example, George J. Stigler, "Regulation: The Confusion of Ends and Means," in Richard L. Landau, ed., *Regulating New Drugs* (Chicago, Ill.: University of Chicago Center for Policy Study, 1973), pp. 9-20. For a more general and comprehensive discussion of this question, see Roger G. Noll, "Government Administrative Behavior and Technological Innovation," California Institute of Technology, Social Science Working Paper No. 62, 1975.

society's view. It is necessary to investigate the expected outcomes of alternative policies, as well as comparing the benefits
and costs that these alternative policies produce.

Several recent studies have begun this task of assessing the
effects of alternative regulatory policies. A number of analytical
studies have been performed on the effects of the 1962 Kefauver
amendments to the Food, Drug, and Cosmetic Act. As back-
ground for the discussion of the analytical studies on regulatory
assessment, the nature of FDA regulatory interactions with the
discovery, development, and marketing of new drugs is considered
in what follows.

FDA Regulation of Drug Development and Introduction

The initial phase of drug discovery involves a team effort among
chemists, biologists, pharmacologists, and others in screening
various molecular structures of potential therapeutic value. The
testing of a drug's pharmacological activity and toxicity is done
first in animals. On the basis of the animal tests, some relatively
small fraction of the compounds that have been screened will be
selected as sufficiently promising to warrant clinical testing on
human subjects. The first phase of human testing is oriented
toward examining a drug's possible adverse effects and is usually
performed on healthy individuals under highly monitored situations. If the firm decides that further testing is warranted, the
drug is then employed in the next phase on a relatively limited
number of patients in controlled studies in order to obtain a
preliminary evaluation of its effectiveness. The third or final
phase involves expanded studies in large patient populations in
order to establish the statistical significance of the drug's efficacy
as well as to uncover rarer side effects.

The end result of all this clinical testing, when it is successful,
is a new drug with therapeutic properties that have sufficient
market value to warrant commercial introduction. Since 1938,
when the Food, Drug, and Cosmetic Act was passed, all new drugs
have been required to undergo a pre-market approval process.
The drug firms must submit to the FDA a new drug application
(NDA) that presents the scientific evidence attesting to the new
compound's safety. Under the 1938 statute, unless the FDA
rejected a new drug compound within a limited period of time
(sixty days), the new compound was automatically approved for
commercial consumption.

In 1962, Congress passed the Kefauver-Harris amendments to the Food, Drug, and Cosmetic Act. These amendments extended the mandate and regulatory control of the FDA in several ways. First, they required firms to provide documented scientific evidence on a new drug's *efficacy* in addition to the proof of *safety* required by the 1938 act. In many instances this has led to a substantial increase in the number of tests required. Second, the amendments gave the FDA, for the first time, discretionary power over the clinical research process. For example, before any tests on humans, firms now are required to submit a new-drug investigational plan (IND) giving the results of animal tests and proposing the research protocols for human tests. On the basis of its evaluation of the IND and the subsequent reports of research findings, the FDA may prohibit or halt clinical research believed to pose excessive risks to human volunteer subjects or believed not to follow sound scientific procedures. Third, the amendments imposed regulatory controls on the advertising and promotion of prescription drugs. In particular, firms must restrict advertising claims to those approved by the FDA in labeling and package inserts.

In addition to these new requirements, there is also evidence that FDA regulatory reviews of drug safety have become more stringent in the post-amendment period than they were before. Contributing to this was the effective repeal of the automatic approval clause of the 1938 law. Over the post-1962 period, therefore, there has been a significant increase in the extent and degree of regulatory controls over ethical drugs. Not only have regulatory reviews of safety apparently become more stringent than they had been, but the FDA has also become directly involved with the innovational process from quite early stages of development through marketing activities.

From a scientific viewpoint, the more stringent regulatory climate that has come about since 1962 provides one frame of reference for empirically evaluating the effects (positive and negative) of increased regulatory controls. Time-series analysis can be undertaken of changes between the pre- and post-amendment period. Similarly, because the regulations were not concurrently adopted in other countries, international comparisons can provide insights into the impact of these regulatory changes. Of course, in either kind of analysis, one must analytically separate the effects of regulation from other important factors that produce parallel or opposing outcomes.

A critique of several recent empirical studies is presented in the next four chapters. Following the analysis of these studies in these chapters, the final chapter is devoted to a discussion of possible policy changes and alternatives to current regulatory procedures.

CHAPTER II

STUDIES OF THE EFFECTS
OF REGULATION
ON DRUG INNOVATION

There is little doubt that the rate of new product introductions in the drug industry has declined drastically over recent years. There is considerable doubt, however, about the nature and cause of the decline. This chapter examines the major hypotheses advanced about that decline as well as the analytical studies that have attempted to explain the role of increased regulation and other factors in this observed decline.

Trends in New Product Innovation

A beginning point for much of the empirical work on the effects of regulation is the time-series data on annual new product innovation for the drug industry. Table 1 shows the annual number of new chemical entities (NCEs) approved by the FDA over the period 1950–1975. New chemical entities are the most relevant category of new products for our current purposes because they represent new compounds not previously marketed and include nearly all major therapeutic advances.[1] New products that are not NCEs involve combinations of existing products, new dosage forms, or new brand names.

Despite year-to-year fluctuations, the trend in NCEs over recent years is clearly downward. As noted above, the Kefauver amendments were enacted in 1962 and the post-amendment

---

[1] The exceptions are new applications for old chemical entities of which lidocaine and propranolol are good examples. See William M. Wardell and Louis Lasagna, *Regulation and Drug Development* (Washington, D.C.: American Enterprise Institute for Public Policy Research, 1975), p. 61.

Table 1

ANNUAL FDA APPROVALS OF NEW CHEMICAL ENTITIES, 1950–1975

Year	Total NCEs [a]	NCEs Excluding Salts [b]	Year	Total NCEs [a]	NCEs Excluding Salts [b]
1950	44	33	1963	13	12
1951	55	47	1964	25	19
1952	40	37	1965	23	18
1953	73	55	1966	18	16
1954	60	36	1967	23	18
1955	57	44	1968	7	7
1956	52	44	1969	12	10
1957	73	53	1970	17	17
1958	45	32	1971	17	13
1959	76	56	1972	11	9
1960	55	47	1973	18	17
1961	43	36	1974	16	16
1962	30	26	1975	12	12

a This list contains compounds that are not truly NCEs (for example, salts and esters of previously marketed drugs). Also, a spot check of these lists indicates that they contain duplicate listings and some omissions; this does not, however, change the basic points contained in the text.
b Excludes salts or esters of previously marketed drugs.
Sources: Data compiled by FDA; lists of drugs presented in Appendix A of testimony by Alexander Schmidt to U.S. Senate Subcommittee on Health of the Committee on Labor and Public Welfare, *Hearings on Legislation Amending the Public Health Service Act and the Federal Food, Drug, and Cosmetic Act,* 93d Congress (Washington, D.C.: U.S. Government Printing Office, 1974), pp. 3077-3103; list of drugs for 1974 and 1975 from Edward R. Nida, *FDA New Drug Approval List* (Washington, D.C.: Office of Public Affairs of the Food and Drug Administration (various dates), a weekly pamphlet.

period in particular has been characterized by a sharp decline in NCEs. Since 1962, the average annual rate of new chemical entities introduced has been seventeen, whereas for the pre-amendment period 1950–1961, the annual rate of new chemical entities introduced was fifty-six.[2]

[2] Since the amendments were passed in late 1962, there is some question whether the post-amendment period should include this year or start with 1963. Research studies summarized in the text adopt different conventions in this regard. In the comparison above (and presumably other analyses as well), the results are little altered by treating 1962 or 1963 as the beginning

This decline in innovation over recent periods has not necessarily been caused by the more stringent regulatory climate. Another hypothesis receiving serious attention in the literature is that the underlying stock of research opportunities was depleted by the rapid rate of innovation occurring in the earlier part of the post-World War II period, and that we are currently on a "plateau" of knowledge. As FDA Commissioner Alexander Schmidt puts it,

> That reason begins with the fact that in many areas of biomedical knowledge, we are on a plateau. We have temporarily exhausted the exploitation of known concepts and tools. Truly dramatic new progress in medicine now waits on some basic innovation in molecular science, some breakthrough in our understanding of disease mechanisms, some new therapeutic concept or some new tool.[3]

Commissioner Schmidt, in testimony before a congressional committee, presents data on yearly marketing of NCEs since 1960 in four countries (the United States, England, France, and West Germany) in order to demonstrate that other countries have also experienced significant declines in the marketing of new NCEs. Figure 1 shows this information, which is compiled using data from Paul de Haen. Commissioner Schmidt argues that because the decline in the 1960s is worldwide, it cannot be attributed simply to regulatory changes that occurred in the United States. Rather, it must have a more fundamental cause—such as the depletion in basic research opportunities. This contention is discussed below.

A second important question concerns the nature of the recent decline in NCEs. Since one of the main additions of the 1962 regulations was the "proof of efficacy" requirement, some decline in NCEs was to be expected if the law worked as intended in screening out ineffective drugs. However, it would be surprising if this fact alone could explain a large portion of the decline: for that to be the case, a large percentage of the new drugs introduced in the pre-amendment period would have to have been ineffective. A few studies to be discussed later suggest, in fact,

---

of the post-amendment period. In my own analysis of the effects of the 1962 amendments on research and development productivity, summarized in the last section of this chapter, this was certainly found to be the case.

[3] Alexander Schmidt, presentation at the American Cancer Society's Writers' Seminar, St. Augustine, Florida, March 1974.

Figure 1

ANNUAL MARKETING OF NCEs IN UNITED STATES, ENGLAND, FRANCE, AND GERMANY

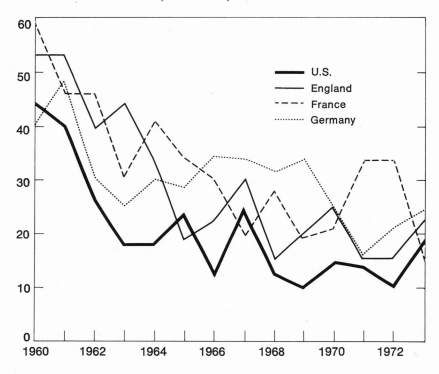

Source: Compiled from data of Paul de Haen and presented as part of FDA Commissioner Alexander Schmidt's testimony before Senate Subcommittee on Health, p. 3051 (see complete reference in Table 1 above).

that only a relatively small percentage of NCE introductions in the pre-amendment period could be classified as ineffective.

The FDA has suggested a second and quite different hypothesis concerning the nature of the decline in NCEs—this being that the decline has been concentrated in drugs that may be classified as having little or no therapeutic gain over existing drugs. In Commissioner Schmidt's testimony, all of the NCEs introduced in the United States are further classified according to whether they represent important, modest, or little (or no) gain over previously existing agents. Figure 2 shows a plot of yearly approvals by therapeutic gain since 1950. On the basis of these data, Commissioner Schmidt concludes:

It is apparent that the decline has been far greater for those drugs representing little or no therapeutic gain than it has been for drugs representing modest or major therapeutic advances. An important fact is that these latter drugs have been developed and approved at a more or less constant rate since the mid-1950s.[4]

The FDA position is therefore that (1) the decline in NCEs has been caused primarily by factors other than regulation and further that (2) it has been concentrated in drugs that represent little or no important therapeutic gain. While this position may have merit, the descriptive statistics that have been offered in its support are hardly compelling.

To begin with the first point, it may be noted that the fact that sizable declines in NCEs have occurred in other countries is not inconsistent with an independent effect of regulation on new drug introductions in the United States. It does suggest that increased regulation is not the only factor producing such declines in the United States, but it does not necessarily support the FDA position that regulation is not the primary factor here.

In interpreting these international data, it should be kept in mind that regulatory controls over new drug introductions also increased significantly in these three European countries in the early 1960s.[5] This was largely a response to the thalidomide incident that directly affected these countries. It is true that none of these countries instituted regulatory control systems as strin-

---

[4] U.S. Congress, Senate, Subcommittee on Health of the Committee on Labor and Public Welfare, *Hearings on Legislation Amending the Public Health Service Act and the Federal Food, Drug, and Cosmetic Act,* 93d Congress (Washington, D.C.: U.S. Government Printing Office, August 1974), pp. 30-49.

[5] The 1969 OECD study on pharmaceuticals notes in this regard:

> The majority of regulations with respect to the manufacture and distribution of medicines are of fairly recent date. Prior to 1960, most countries had little more than a basal system of factory inspection, often combined with simple procedure for the registrations of specialities, and sometimes coupled with general regulations on quality (analogous to those applicable to foodstuffs) and official or voluntary regulation of advertising and prescription.
> The rapid development of drug laws from around 1960 onwards was prompted by the conviction that the large measure of freedom to make and sell medicines could result in considerable risk to public health, the more so because the recent advances towards more specific and more effective, often synthetic, drugs entailed a growing inherent danger of untoward effects connected with their use. The new laws were directed firstly to the *safety* of drugs, secondly to their *efficacy,* thirdly (in some countries) to the manner of their *promotion,* and fourthly (in a few countries) to their *pricing.*

(Organization of Economic Cooperation and Development, *Pharmaceuticals: Gaps in Technology* [Paris: OECD, 1969], p. 88.)

Figure 2

FDA CLASSIFICATION OF ANNUAL NEW DRUG APPROVALS
BY DEGREE OF THERAPEUTIC IMPORTANCE, 1950–1973

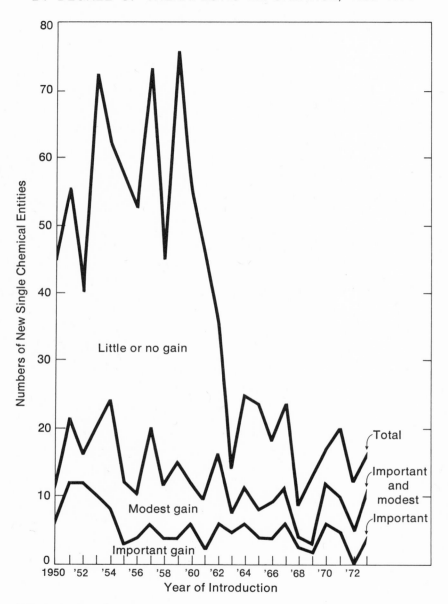

Source: Same as Figure 1, but p. 3052.

gent or extensive in scope as those put into effect in the United States in 1962. Nevertheless, it would have been surprising if declining trends in NCE introductions were not also observed abroad, given the regulatory changes that did occur there in the early 1960s. The data in Figure 1 do show much lower absolute rates of introductions in the United States than abroad over the entire period. This is consistent with the notion that drug regulation, while increasing both here and abroad since the early 1960s, has remained *relatively* more stringent in the United States.

It is also important to bear in mind that the number of foreign introductions is itself not independent of the United States regulatory environment. Given the multinational nature of the pharmaceutical industry, it is reasonable to expect that increased regulation in the United States would produce a "spillover" or "echo" effect on the level of NCE introductions abroad. U.S. firms collectively have a large share of the total ethical drug sales in the countries shown in Figure 1.[6] If more stringent regulation in the United States increases the research and development costs of U.S. firms and lowers their rates of pharmaceutical discovery and innovation, their level of NCE introductions will tend to decline not only in the United States but also worldwide. Similarly, foreign multinational firms market many of their drugs in the United States, and their U.S. sales represent an important component of their overall revenues for many new drugs. Hence, the rate of return to drug discovery and innovation for foreign firms also will be adversely affected by significant increases in the costs of introducing new drugs in the United States. The adverse effect tends to produce a lower rate of NCE introductions in foreign countries. Thus, at least part of the reduced rate of NCE introductions abroad may be viewed as a direct consequence of increased regulation in the United States. Some empirical evidence that is consistent with the hypothesis of an "echo" effect of U.S. drug regulation on foreign introductions will be discussed in Chapter IV.

The second basic point made by the FDA, that the decline in NCEs in the United States has largely been in drugs that represent

---

[6] For example, John Vernon and I have calculated that U.S. firms had between 38 and 47 percent of total U.K. ethical drug sales over the period 1962 to 1974 and comparable shares of innovational output over portions of this period. See Henry G. Grabowski and John M. Vernon, "Structural Effects of Regulation in the Drug Industry," in Robert Masson and P. David Qualls, eds., *Essays on Industrial Organization in Honor of Joe Bain* (Cambridge: Ballinger, 1976), pp. 181-205.

minor therapeutic advances, is also subject to debate and qualification. The FDA provides no real discussion of the criteria used to classify the drugs by therapeutic gain. A number of expert rankings of new drugs have appeared in recent years—including four lists emanating from the FDA (Table 2) and a number from academic sources.[7] There is a wide variance in these expert rankings—even among the four lists from the FDA. Whether significant shifts in the composition of NCEs have occurred over time is clearly a question deserving further analysis. It will be discussed below in the context of some of the specific studies surveyed.

From a broader perspective it should also be noted that even if the FDA's second hypothesis were correct, it would not necessarily imply that social welfare will be unchanged by a lessened rate of introduction of NCEs. The introduction of new products that represent relatively small incremental advances over existing products can over time have a large cumulative impact on social welfare. Furthermore, as Professor Oates emphasizes in testimony before the Kennedy hearings, there are also a number of drugs whose main use or novel action was discovered only after market introduction (and not from animal models or even clinical trials). Hence any procedure that reduces the total flow of NCEs to the market will also tend to reduce this serendipitous but highly important method of progress.[8] Finally, the greater the number of independent sources of drugs with similar properties on the market at any given time, the greater the likelihood of competition by price cuts that will convey direct benefits to consumers.

In summary, one cannot resolve the fundamental questions at stake here by simple descriptive statistics that only count and classify NCE introductions in the United States and abroad. There are, however, a number of recent academic studies that attempt to move from the comparison of descriptive statistics to the formulation of models capable of testing alternative hypotheses

---

[7] Alternative classifications of new drugs by therapeutic importance from non-FDA sources have been employed by Jerome E. Schnee, "Innovation and Discovery in the Ethical Pharmaceutical Industry," in Edwin Mansfield, ed., *Research and Innovation in the Modern Corporation* (New York: W. W. Norton, 1971) and George Teeling-Smith, "Comparative International Sources of Innovation," in Joseph D. Cooper, ed., *Regulation, Economics, and Pharmaceutical Innovation* (Washington, D.C.: American University, 1976), pp. 59-68.

[8] John Oates, M.D., testimony before U.S. Senate Subcommittee on Health of the Committee on Labor and Public Welfare, *Hearings on Regulation of New Drug R & D by the Food and Drug Administration, 1974*, 93d Congress (Washington, D.C.: U.S. Government Printing Office, 1974), pp. 658-661.

Table 2
FOUR FDA ASSESSMENTS OF IMPORTANT THERAPEUTIC
ADVANCES, 1950–1973

Year Drug Introduced	Number of Drugs Deemed Important				Range
	1971	1972	1973	1974	
1950	6	3	3	6	3 - 6
1951	6	5	6	11	5 - 11
1952	14	12	13	12	12 - 14
1953	10	6	7	9	6 - 10
1954	8	5	10	8	5 - 10
1955	14	6	5	3	3 - 14
1956	10	4	4	4	4 - 10
1957	13	9	10	6	6 - 13
1958	12	5	6	4	4 - 12
1959	21	8	9	4	4 - 21
1960	15	6	8	6	6 - 15
1961	15	4	4	2	2 - 15
1962	16	7	7	6	6 - 16
1963	10	4	6	5	4 - 10
1964	10	7	8	5	5 - 10
1965	12	5	7	4	4 - 12
1966	8	4	5	4	4 - 8
1967	12	8	9	6	6 - 12
1968	9	5	4	3	3 - 9
1969	4	2	2	1	1 - 4
1970	8	4	6	6	4 - 8
1971	—	5	5	5	5
1972	—	—	—	0	n.a.
1973	—	—	—	2	n.a.

Sources: 1971 assessment—W. McVicker, "New Drug Development Study: Final Report," unpublished report for the Department of Health, Education, and Welfare; 1972 assessment—H. Simmons presentation, FDA National Advisory Committee meeting, September 28, 1972; 1973 assessment—H. Simmons testimony, Nelson Subcommittee Hearings, February 5, 1973; 1974 assessment—Commissioner Schmidt testimony, Kennedy Subcommittee Hearings, as noted in Table 1.

about the observed decline in NCEs. These studies are described and criticized in the discussion that follows.

Martin Baily's Study

The first published statistical analysis of the effects of the 1962 amendments on the rate of innovation is by Martin Baily.[9] Using

[9] Martin Neil Baily, "Research and Development Cost and Returns: The U.S. Pharmaceutical Industry," *Journal of Political Economy,* vol. 80, no. 1 (January-February 1972), pp. 70-85.

a "production function" model of drug development, Baily postulates that the number of new chemical entities (of industry origin) introduced in any period will be a function of (1) past research and development expenditures by the industry, (2) the stringency of FDA regulations, and (3) the depletion of the stock of research opportunities available to the industry. Using this type of model, he analyzes the number of new product introductions for the industry over the period 1954 to 1969.

His model explains 95 percent of the variance in the ratio of industry NCEs to research and development expenditures over the period from 1954 to 1969. The variables measuring regulatory "tightness" and the depletion of research opportunities have the postulated effect and are statistically significant. The regulatory variable also exhibits a large quantitative impact in explaining the observed decline in NCEs per research and development dollar invested. In particular Baily finds that the level of research and development expenditures necessary to generate a given flow of new products is more than doubled as a result of the 1962 amendments.

A potential problem in the Baily analysis is that both the effects of regulation and the effects of research depletion are measured by proxy variables, and are therefore subject to considerable measurement error. Regulatory tightness is represented by a simple intercept shift—a "dummy" variable that takes the value one over the post-1962 period and zero in the pre-1962 period. The depletion of research opportunities is measured by a lagged seven-year moving average of NCEs introduced in the United States from all sources. It is quite possible that the effects of regulation and research depletion may be confounded when they are measured by these aggregate proxy variables. Furthermore, the model does not explicitly allow for additions to the stock of knowledge over the period, although the moving average formulation for research depletion might implicitly capture some changes in this regard.

Since the Baily model was published, five additional years of data have become available. To check on the stability of his model, I reestimated his basic equation over the longer period, 1954 to 1974. The estimated coefficients for the proxy variables on regulation and depletion continue to have the predicted negative signs. However, the coefficient on the depletion variable now becomes statistically insignificant and the explanatory power of the model for the longer period declines (to be exact, the R^2 decreases from 0.95 to 0.86).[10]

The proxy variable employed by Baily for research depletion thus turns out to be unstable when his analysis is extended forward in time. Given the poor statistical performance of this variable and the elusive nature of the concept itself, the development of alternative means of separating regulatory from non-regulatory factors would seem desirable. Later in this chapter we will discuss an alternative approach for statistically separating the effects of regulation from other factors, such as research depletion. It is based on an international comparative analysis of trends in NCEs per research and development dollar invested in the United States and in the United Kingdom. This analysis is part of a forthcoming study carried out by the author in collaboration with John Vernon and Lacy Thomas.[11]

Sam Peltzman's Study

The effects of the 1962 amendments on the rate of drug innovation are also investigated in a study by Sam Peltzman.[12] His analysis is part of a general cost-benefit analysis of the amendments. In this section of our study here, only his analysis of the effect of the amendments on the rate and character of drug innovation will be considered. In Chapter V, the methods he employs to calculate the benefits and costs of these effects to consumers will be discussed along with other cost-benefit studies.

While Baily's study is based on a production function analysis and emphasizes supply-side factors, Peltzman's model focuses on the demand side. A basic operating assumption in Peltzman's analysis is that the supply of NCEs in any period will adjust over time to the expected market size and demand for prescription drugs. New drugs are treated as homogenous commodities and shifts in demand are the exogenous variables to which this

---

[10] For a further discussion of these findings, see Henry G. Grabowski, John M. Vernon, and Lacy G. Thomas, "The Effects of Regulatory Policy on the Incentives to Innovate: An International Comparative Analysis"; Samuel A. Mitchell and Emery A. Link, eds., *Impact of Public Policy on Drug Innovation and Pricing* (Washington, D.C.: American University, 1976), pp. 47-82.

[11] Ibid.

[12] Sam Peltzman, "The Benefits and Costs of New Drug Development" in Landau, *Regulating New Drugs,* pp. 113-212; also Sam Peltzman, *Regulation of Pharmaceutical Innovation: The 1962 amendments* (Washington, D.C.: American Enterprise Institute for Public Policy Research, 1974).

homogenous supply of new drugs responds (with a lag). This is essentially a "demand-pull" model of technological change. It builds on the approach of Jacob Schmookler, who postulated that technological innovation generally followed demand rather than the other way around.[13] In his economic work, Peltzman uses moving averages of total out-of-hospital prescriptions and personal consumption expenditures on physicians' services as demand variables determining the flow of new chemical entities in each period. His model also includes cumulative NCEs lagged one year as an explanatory variable to take account of dynamic adjustment effects.

A "residual" approach is employed to calculate the impact of the 1962 amendments. The model is first estimated on pre-amendment data (1948–1962), on which it provides a relatively good fit to the data ($R^2 = .80$). The estimated coefficients from this regression are then used to predict what the number of NCEs would have been in each year in the absence of the 1962 amendments. The effects of the 1962 amendments are then calculated as the residual difference in the predicted and actual flow of NCEs in each year in the post-amendment period.

On the basis of this residual analysis, Peltzman presents the following results:

> I conclude from these data that: a) The 1962 Amendments significantly reduced the flow of new chemical entities and, what is perhaps more interesting, b) all of the observed difference between the pre- and the post-1962 New Chemical Entities flow can be attributed to the 1962 Amendments.[14]

In effect, Peltzman's model suggests that the rate of innovation in the post-amendment period is more than halved as a result of the 1962 amendments. However, his model never formally includes supply-side factors relating to the depletion of scientific knowledge, as suggested by the "plateau of knowledge" theory, although it may implicitly capture some of these effects through the inclusion of lagged cumulative NCE introductions as an explanatory variable. Nevertheless, given that the effects of regulation are captured only indirectly through the "residual" procedure, the effects of depletion of knowledge could obviously also be reflected in this residual if they were contemporaneous

---

[13] Jacob Schmookler, *Invention and Economic Growth* (Cambridge, Mass.: Harvard University Press, 1966).

[14] Peltzman, "Benefits and Costs," p. 126.

in nature. This is a point on which further research would appear warranted.

Peltzman next performs a fairly extensive investigation to estimate what portion of the decline in NCEs might be classified as a decline in the introduction of ineffective drugs deterred by the "proof of efficacy" requirement in the new law. One form of analysis involves a comparison of the growth rates of new drugs in the pre- and post-amendment periods. This analysis is based on a consumer (doctor and patient) learning effect concerning the effectiveness of new drugs—that is, if it turns out that a new drug is ineffective, one should find a decline in its market share over time as patients and their doctors gain experience with the drug. Thus some information on the relative incidence of ineffective drugs in the pre- and post-amendment periods can be inferred from analysis of growth-rate patterns in the two periods. Peltzman also examines expert evaluations of drug efficacy (for example, those of the AMA) in the pre- and post-amendment periods to obtain another perspective on this question.

On the basis of this analysis Peltzman concludes that a relatively small portion of NCEs in the pre-amendment period were ineffective—at most something on the order of 10 percent of total new drug introductions.[15] Moreover, his analysis of evaluations by medical experts suggests that the proportion of ineffective drugs has remained roughly the same in the pre-1962 and post-1962 periods. Given that the rate of new drug introductions was more than halved in the post-amendment period, his analysis therefore suggests that a large decline took place in effective drugs.

Peltzman's data may be used to determine whether the decline in NCEs has been concentrated in drugs that represent little or no gain over existing drugs, as conjectured by the FDA. His analysis shows not only that there was a sharp decline in the number of NCEs in the post-amendment period, but also that there was a roughly parallel decline in the total sales and market share captured by new drugs over this period. Each NCE on average gained approximately the same share (one-tenth of 1 percent) of total prescriptions in both periods.[16] This fact is difficult to reconcile with the FDA's assertion that the decline in NCEs has been concentrated in drugs representing little or no gain, while the number of therapeutically important new drugs introduced

---

[15] Ibid., pp. 161-170.
[16] Ibid., p. 125.

has not decreased significantly. If this were so, one would expect the average market share of new drugs to rise over time, to reflect the larger proportion of new drugs representing important therapeutic gains—unless, of course, there were no correlation between the importance of a drug's therapeutic gain and its market share and sales. This possible lack of correlation does not seem very plausible intuitively, and this set of results therefore casts some doubt on the FDA claim that the decline in NCEs has been concentrated in drugs with minor therapeutic gains.

Comparative International Analyses

International analysis of innovational activity might ultimately provide the best means of separating the effects of changes in regulation from the effects of other factors operating concurrently. Innovational activities in all countries would be commonly affected by such specific forces as a depletion in basic scientific opportunities, whereas regulatory procedures often differ significantly among countries. An analysis of this sort is therefore the closest thing available to a natural experiment for gauging the effects of these variables. Of course, it differs from a completely controlled experiment insofar as the levels of introductions abroad are not completely independent of the U.S. regulatory climate, as I noted above.

International comparative analyses of drug regulation are performed in a series of papers by William Wardell, a clinical pharmacologist. In these papers, Wardell investigates market introduction of NCEs in the United States and the United Kingdom over the period since 1962.[17] Because Wardell's work focuses only on the post-amendment period, it is not entirely an analysis of the effects of the 1962 amendments. It is rather an analysis of two alternative systems of regulation and of their total effect on the introduction of new drugs. The changes embodied in the 1962 amendments are, of course, among the main differences between the two systems in the post-1962 period. However, other factors differentiate the two systems, and many of these predate the 1962 amendments. Nevertheless, this kind of inter-country analysis is, scientifically or from a policy perspective, no less interesting than an investigation addressed to the specific impact

---

[17] An updated and somewhat condensed version of these papers appears in Wardell and Lasagna, *Regulation and Drug Development*, Chapters VII through IX.

of the 1962 amendments. Moreover, in principle, one could extend these international analyses backward in time and also examine differences before 1962. Some initial work along these lines is presented in the next section.

Before I discuss Wardell's findings, it will be appropriate to discuss the major similarities and differences between the U.S. and U.K. regulatory systems in the post-1962 period. Both systems required formal pre-market safety reviews over the entire time period. However, while the United States added a proof-of-efficacy standard in 1962, the United Kingdom did not adopt any formal requirement until the Medicines Act became effective in 1971. As a result of the 1962 amendments, the United States also required an IND filing before any clinical testing on human volunteers or patients, whereas the United Kingdom had a voluntary—but apparently effective—IND procedure (just for patients) only since 1967. The IND filing became compulsory in 1971 under the U.K. Medicines Act.

Perhaps even more important than differences in legal requirements are the differences in the institutional characteristics of the review process. These differences were apparently intensified in the wake of the thalidomide incident in the early 1960s. Sir Derrick Dunlop, who was chairman of the British Committee on Safety of Medicines for many years, provides a detailed comparison of the two systems in a recent conference on drug regulation. He notes:

> The main difference between the two systems is that ultimate power to license medicines in the United Kingdom rests with the Licensing Authority (the Ministers responsible to Parliament) acting on the professional advice of the Safety Committees. The decisions of these committees are taken by professional men whose careers in no way depend on their membership of the committees on which they serve part time in a virtually honorary capacity as an altruistic chore. They are assisted, of course, by a small staff of expert professional civil servants who do most of the preparatory work, but the decisions are taken by the committees. It is probable that the experience gained from the eight years' informal Safety of Drugs Committee will tincture their subsequent official actions.

> In the United States, on the other hand, ultimate power rests with the full time professional civil servants of the FDA whose careers depend on the correctness of their

decisions, and who are subject to formidable grillings by Congressional Committees. The FDA has to work under fairly rigid rules by Congress which seem to rely more on animal experiments than is usual in the United Kingdom.[18]

The greater use of external professional advice in the United Kingdom apparently has produced a regulatory incentive structure less prone to bias in the direction of caution and delay than the structure in the United States. This, combined with very different policies on proof of efficacy, has meant a system with shorter review times and lower development costs than in the United States.

One dimension in which the United Kingdom has apparently had regulatory controls more stringent than those in the United States is in the area of post-marketing surveillance. According to Wardell, post-marketing surveillance is far more seriously undertaken in the United Kingdom than in the United States.[19] The British system therefore apparently combines a less bureaucratic pre-market screening process for new drugs (one that relies more on medical judgment than in the United States) with stronger post-market checks.

Wardell's first paper examines drug innovation in the United States and United Kingdom for nine therapeutic classes over the period 1962–1971.[20] For this period he finds that the number of new chemical entities introduced into the United Kingdom was roughly 50 percent higher than the number introduced into the United States (159 NCEs compared to 103 for the United States). Moreover, for the drugs that were mutually available in both countries by 1971, twice as many were introduced first in the United Kingdom as were introduced first in the United States. This "drug lag" was found to be the greatest in the areas of cardiovascular, gastrointestinal, and respiratory medicine, and diuretic and antibacterial therapy.

In a second paper, Wardell surveys British and American doctors to gain some perspective on the British usage and American awareness of drugs in five therapeutic classes (where a lag

---

[18] Derrick Dunlop, "The British System of Drug Regulation" in Landau, *Regulating New Drugs*, pp. 229-238.

[19] Wardell and Lasagna, *Regulation and Drug Development*, p. 106.

[20] William M. Wardell, "Introduction of New Therapeutic Drugs in the United States and Great Britain: An International Comparison," *Clinical Pharmacology and Therapeutics*, vol. 14, no. 5 (September-October 1973), pp. 773-790.

in U.S. introductions had been found).[21] These survey results indicate that certain drugs currently unavailable in the United States were widely prescribed by United Kingdom physicians (and in some cases were the drugs of choice for certain conditions). In addition, physicians surveyed at a leading U.S. teaching hospital were unaware of many of these drugs, although in cases when they were aware of them, they generally expressed a desire to have the particular drug available in the United States.

In a third paper, Wardell attempts to assess the therapeutic consequences of this different rate of introduction through a detailed discussion of the individual drugs available in the two countries.[22] He concludes:

> From the present study, it is clear that each country has gained in some ways and lost in others. On balance, however, it is difficult to argue that the United States has escaped an inordinate amount of new-drug toxicity by its conservative approach; it has gained little else in return. On the contrary, it is relatively easy to show that Britain has gained by having effective drugs available sooner. Furthermore, the cost of this policy in terms of damage due to adverse drug reactions have been small compared with the existing levels of damage produced by older drugs. There appear to be no other therapeutic costs of any consequence to Britain. In view of the clear benefits demonstrable from some of the drugs introduced into Britain, it appears that the United States has, on balance, lost more than it has gained from adopting a more conservative approach than did Britain in the post-thalidomide era.[23]

In a paper presented to the 1974 AEI Conference on Drug Development and Marketing, Wardell extends his analyses to cover the period from the beginning of 1972 to the middle of 1974.[24] This recent period was of particular interest because in 1971 (as noted above) a new law, the Medicines Act, took effect

21 William M. Wardell, "British Usage and American Awareness of Some New Therapeutic Drugs," Clinical Pharmacology and Therapeutics, vol. 14, no. 6 (November-December 1973), pp. 1022-1034.

22 William M. Wardell, "Therapeutic Implications of the Drug Lag," Clinical Pharmacology and Therapeutics, vol. 15, no. 1 (January 1974), pp. 73-96.

23 Ibid., p. 90.

24 William M. Wardell, "Developments in the Introduction of New Drugs in the United States and Britain, 1971-1974," in Robert B. Helms, ed., Drug Development and Marketing (Washington, D.C.: American Enterprise Institute for Public Policy Research, 1975), pp. 165-182.

in Britain, making the review process more formal in nature than it had been. At the same time, there have been some efforts over recent years to change organizational procedures in the United States to reduce delays and make reviews more efficient. All of this is to say that there has been some tendency, as yet of relatively minor proportions, for the two systems to converge.

Wardell observes some significant changes from his earlier results. Most notably, the United States did reduce or remove the differences in drug availability in a number of therapeutic categories. This was not true, however, in all cases, with anti-hypertensive therapy and diuretics being areas where the United States was found to be still noticeably behind the United Kingdom.[25] Nevertheless, Wardell's overall findings on the most recent data are more positive than his findings in his earlier work and suggest that the U.S. pattern of drug availability may be coming to be more in accordance with current world standards of professional and scientific thought.

Grabowski, Vernon, and Thomas Study

In a recently completed study, John Vernon, Lacy Thomas, and I attempt to isolate the effects of increased regulation from non-regulatory factors on drug innovation through a comparative analysis of the United States and United Kingdom over the pre- and post-amendment period.[26] In particular, we estimate a production-function model similar to Martin Baily's model discussed above. However, instead of trying to measure research depletion through a moving average of past introductions, we attempt to separate regulatory from nonregulatory factors through a comparative analysis of developments in the United States and United Kingdom.

The dependent variable in Baily's model is in effect a productivity measure—the number of new chemical entities (of industry origin) introduced annually in the United States per

---

[25] This finding is of some interest inasmuch as in a recent report of the FDA commissioner, the director of the FDA's Bureau of Drugs acknowledged that the cardio-pulmonary division of the FDA had been having difficulties with medical officers who had been too conservative in their review of new drug applications. See U.S. Food and Drug Administration, *Annual Report 1975* (Washington, D.C.: U.S. Government Printing Office, 1976), pp. 598-599.

[26] Grabowski, Vernon, and Thomas, "The Effects of Regulatory Policy on the Incentives to Innovate: International Comparative Analysis" (see note 10 above).

dollar of research and development outlay by the drug industry. We were able to develop a comparable variable for the United Kingdom over the period 1960 to 1971.[27] Our formal analysis is based on the premise that nonregulatory factors such as the depletion of research opportunities would influence the productivity of research and development in both countries in similar ways, but that more stringent regulation in the United States would show up as an additional observed effect in the United States but not in the United Kingdom.

International comparative analyses are generally subject to some downward bias in estimating the impact of regulation on innovation, inasmuch as regulatory controls became more stringent in the early 1960s in the United Kingdom as well as the United States. Hence, one is comparing the U.S. experience not with experience in a completely constant regulatory environment in the United Kingdom, but rather with experience in an environment where regulatory controls were also increasing. At best these international comparisons will only track differences in regulatory stringency between the two countries since 1960. Nevertheless, as discussed above, the United Kingdom maintained very different policies from those in the United States for both proof of efficacy and IND requirements (two key aspects of the 1962 amendments) until the Medicines Act was put into effect in 1971. Hence, the effect of these particular policy differences should be reflected in our analysis of the 1960–1971 period.

In addition, some downward bias in estimating the impact of regulation occurs because adverse impact on innovation resulting from increased regulation in the United States will have some tendency to spill over to other countries and result in lower NCE introductions abroad as well. However, in our analysis, this source of downward bias is minimized by the fact that the dependent variable is a research and development productivity measure rather than the absolute level of introductions. Regulatory changes in one country can be expected to have much less impact on shifts in the research and development production function in other countries than on the absolute level of introductions. Thus, while our analysis tends to understate the effects of regulation on innovation (for this and for other reasons as well),

---

[27] 1960 was the earliest year for which we were able to obtain data on U.K. introductions; 1971 was selected as the terminal year to avoid confounding the trends with increased regulation in the United Kingdom in 1971. For further details, see the discussion in "The Effects of Regulatory Policy on the Incentives to Innovate," pp. 63-70.

the bias is minimized by our use of research and development productivity as the dependent variable.

A principal finding from our analysis is that U.S. research and development "productivity" declined about six-fold between 1960–1961 and 1966–1970. The decrease in the United Kingdom was about threefold. Clearly these figures indicate that research and development productivity has declined significantly, not only in the United States, but in the United Kingdom as well. This is consistent with the hypothesis of a worldwide depletion of research opportunities advanced by FDA Commissioner Schmidt and others. However, declining research and development productivity in the United Kingdom could also reflect a number of additional factors, including increased regulatory controls in the United Kingdom over this period. Further research on this question is warranted.

Given the fact that a much more rapid decline in research and development productivity occurred in the United States than in the United Kingdom between 1960 and 1971, there is support for the position that additional factors were at work in the U.S. case. We attribute this more rapid decline for the United States to differences in regulatory procedures associated with the 1962 amendments. On the basis of a more sophisticated analysis using these results, we further estimate that the 1962 amendments have roughly doubled the cost per NCE. This estimate is actually quite close to that from Martin Baily's earlier study. However, as noted above, the depletion measure used in the original Baily model proved to be unstable when his analysis was extended forward in time and this instability was a primary factor motivating our comparative analysis of international data on research and development productivity.

Our findings are necessarily somewhat tentative in character, given that the analysis is based on the comparison of only two countries and data were available in the United Kingdom for only a few years before 1962. Nevertheless, this general approach would seem to offer considerable promise, and an effort should be made to develop more comprehensive data bases for the United Kingdom and for other countries.

If increased regulation has significantly raised research and development costs and lowered research and development productivity in the United States, one might also expect to observe U.S. multinational firms shifting research and development abroad in an attempt to offset some portion of these increased costs. The incentive to do so would depend on a number of factors (such as FDA policy on foreign tests) that are discussed in detail in the next chapter. The empirical evidence concerning the degree to which firms are actually shifting research and development abroad is also reviewed there along with a number of related developments.

Summary and Conclusions

New product innovation in the ethical drug industry as measured by NCEs has significantly declined in recent years. Roughly proportional decreases also have occurred in new product sales and market shares. It is therefore hard to argue that only the number of relatively unimportant drugs has decreased or that the observed decline is a statistical illusion.

A number of recent studies have investigated the causes of this decline in innovation and, in particular, have investigated the extent to which the decline is related to increased regulatory controls. From a methodological standpoint, it is difficult to sort out the effects of regulation from the effects of other factors. Nevertheless, the studies do provide a number of different analytical approaches to solving this problem. *A consistent finding is that regulation has had a significant negative effect on the rate of innovation.* While each of the individual studies has shortcomings, taken together they would seem to provide considerable support for the hypothesis that regulation has been one of the principal factors responsible for the observed decline in innovation. There is also evidence that nonregulatory factors have had some negative impact on drug innovation, and further analysis, particularly of the research depletion hypothesis, would seem to be warranted.

CHAPTER III

STUDIES OF RETURNS AND SHIFTS IN DRUG RESEARCH AND DEVELOPMENT

In addition to studies investigating the effects of regulation on drug innovation, there have been several related studies of recent developments in research and development. Some of these studies have focused on the profitability of research and development in the ethical drug industry. Others have investigated growth patterns and allocational shifts in research and development here and abroad. These studies and their findings are discussed in this chapter.

Rates of Return to Research and Development Activity

A number of studies point to sharply declining private rates of return to research and development activity in the post-1962 period. This is perhaps not very surprising given the aggregate trends in drug innovation described in the last chapter. Nevertheless, the most recent work in this area suggests expected rates of return on drug research and development that are significantly below the average rate of return on all manufacturers' investment. If this holds true, one would expect to see a shift over time away from domestic research and development expenditures to other activities with more promising rates of return. In the discussion that follows, I shall first examine the findings and methodology of these rate-of-return studies and then turn to their broad implications.

The first analysis of drug-industry returns from research and development expenditures to be considered is by Martin Baily.[1]

---

[1] Baily, "Research and Development," pp. 78-83.

This study was undertaken in conjunction with his production function analysis discussed in Chapter II. Baily calculates rates of return for six large firms. He begins with the estimated production function relating the number of new chemical entities to past levels of research and development expenditures. He then estimates a second functional relation between each firm's profits and past levels of innovational output. Using this two-stage approach, he finds average pre-tax rates of return to drug research in the pre-amendment period (1954–1961) to be approximately 30 percent. He also finds the rate of return to be steadily declining over this period, being an estimated 25 percent in 1961.

Baily's estimated rate of return for the pre-amendment period is somewhat above the average rate of return to all manufacturing investment. This is what one would expect from an investment generally considered to be of above-average "riskiness." Moreover, it conforms to the general results of Mansfield, Griliches, and others who have found above average rates of return to research and development over a large spectrum of industry classes (such as petroleum refining, food products, and wearing apparel).[2] According to these studies, pre-tax rates of return on research and development in excess of 30 percent have not been uncommon.

While Baily does not formally calculate any rates of return for the post-amendment period, he offers the following comments.

> It does not require econometrics to see, however, that 224 new drugs were introduced from 1954 to 1961 and 86.5 from 1962 to 1969, and much more was spent on R and D development. Unless returns per drug are dramatically higher (in excess of the normal growth of the market), then profitability will be much lower. If the same estimated coefficients that were used for the earlier period are applied to returns in the post-1962 period, then the rate of return is somewhat less than half the 1961 level.[3]

Two studies that do calculate rates of return in the post-amendment period are by Harold Clymer and David Schwartzman.[4]

---

[2] See, for example, Edwin Mansfield, *Industrial Research and Technological Innovation* (New York: W. W. Norton, 1968), pp. 65–82, and Zvi Griliches, "Returns to Research and Development in the Private Sector," Harvard University, January 1975, mimeographed.

[3] Baily, "Research and Development," p. 83.

[4] Harold Clymer, "The Economics of Drug Innovation" in M. Pernarowski and M. Darrach, eds., *The Development and Control of New Drug Products*

The discussion here focuses on Schwartzman's study, because it contains a more extensive and more current analysis of this question than Clymer's. However, both studies employ similar methodologies and reach consistent conclusions.

Schwartzman begins his analysis by computing the annual sales revenues generated by the new chemical entities introduced in the United States in the 1966–1972 period. In order to calculate an expected rate of return to discovering and developing these drugs, he has to estimate (1) the level and time pattern of research and development costs incurred to obtain these NCEs, and (2) the current and expected future profits generated by these new product sales.

To calculate costs, Schwartzman takes total industry research and development expenditures and allocates a fixed proportion to the discovery of NCEs according to the findings of previous case studies. He further assumes a ten-year development period, also on the basis of industry case studies. His calculations yield an estimate of $24.4 million of total research and development costs per NCE. This he assumes to be uniformly spread over the ten-year development period.

On the income side, he estimates profit margins on new product sales from aggregate corporate data on six companies that collectively had over 60 percent of total industry sales. The companies were selected because of their high degree of specialization in pharmaceuticals. This procedure yielded an estimated pre-tax profit margin of 25.6 percent. It may be noted that Schwartzman assumes a fifteen-year period as the product life of the average NCE, which is much higher than past case studies would suggest. While the product life may have been shorter in the 1950s and 1960s, his estimate may now be more realistic as a result of the more stringent regulatory climate and the strong decline in the rate of new product introductions.

The estimates of cost and revenues when taken together yield a rate of return of 6.6 percent (before tax). While Schwartzman's analysis obviously embodies a number of critical assumptions, each of which is subject to significant error, his methods, when used to calculate expected rates of return to research and development in 1960, yield results that are generally consistent with Baily's.[5] Baily found a pre-tax return of around 25 percent in

(Vancouver, B.C.: Evergreen Press, 1971), and David Schwartzman, *The Expected Return from Pharmaceutical Research* (Washington, D.C.: American Enterprise Institute for Public Policy Research, 1975).
[5] Baily, "Research and Development," p. 82.

1960 while Schwartzman estimated it to be 22.8 percent. Thus these two studies, which use quite different techniques to obtain rates of return, seem to be in general agreement.

Perhaps the weakest link in Schwartzman's chain of assumptions concerns the calculation of profit margins. His analysis uses data on total corporate activities to estimate average profit margins on new chemical entities. Such a calculation includes older products (some of which no longer have patent protection) as well as products other than ethical drugs. It would seem reasonable to assume that profit margins on new chemical entities would be significantly above the average profit margin earned on all corporate activities.

Schwartzman performs a sensitivity analysis to see how his rate of return calculation changes with different assumptions on profit margins. Other things constant, at a 40-percent profit margin (instead of 25.6 percent), the estimated pre-tax rate of return would increase to 12 percent. This is still a very low rate of return for what is generally considered to be a risky activity.

Using data on the sales of selected new drugs, Schwartzman also investigates the riskiness of new drug development. He performs a rough analysis of the variability in rates of return from new product introductions over the period in question (1962–1968). While a few drugs apparently earned spectacular rates of return (for example, the tranquilizer Valium), some of the largest firms did not have any new drug over this period with sales large enough to be considered a commercial success. In general, the analysis shows a high variability in the sales of new chemical entities: this would suggest that a significant "risk" premium is appropriate for new drug development throughout the post-amendment period examined by Schwartzman.

Given the thrust of the Clymer-Schwartzman findings that the expected rate of return on pharmaceutical research and development is significantly below the rate obtainable on alternative investments, one would expect to observe a decline in real resources devoted to drug research and development and a corresponding shift of these resources to other domestic and foreign activities offering a more promising rate of return. To get some preliminary idea whether this is the case, it is instructive to examine the domestic research and development expenditures of the pharmaceutical industry over time. In Table 3 the relevant data are presented for the period 1961–1974. The first column shows that in absolute dollar terms, the amount of domestic

Table 3

DOMESTIC AND FOREIGN EXPENDITURES OF U.S. ETHICAL DRUG INDUSTRY, 1961–1974 [a]

Year	Domestic R and D, Current Dollars (millions)	Domestic R and D, Constant Dollars [b] (millions)	Ratio of R and D to Sales, Current Dollars [c] (percent)	Foreign R and D, Current Dollars (millions)	Ratio of Foreign R and D to Total R and D (percent)
1961	215.9	215.9	10.4	11.4	5.0
1962	224.8	222.3	9.7	13.0	5.5
1963	248.2	242.4	10.2	18.9	7.1
1964	254.3	244.5	9.8	24.0	8.6
1965	304.2	287.0	10.3	24.5	7.5
1966	344.2	316.1	10.8	30.2	8.1
1967	377.9	336.2	11.1	34.5	8.4
1968	410.4	351.1	10.8	39.1	8.7
1969	464.1	378.8	11.2	41.7	8.2
1970	518.6	401.1	11.7	47.2	8.3
1971	576.5	426.7	12.0	52.3	8.3
1972	600.7	430.0	11.7	66.1	9.9
1973	643.8	436.5	11.4	108.7	14.4
1974	726.0	446.5	11.6	132.5	15.4

[a] For human-use pharmaceutical research and development. (Veterinary-use pharmaceutical R and D is excluded.)
[b] Deflated by GNP price deflator converted to 1961 base.
[c] Domestic R and D and sales only.
Source: Pharmaceutical Manufacturers Association, *Annual Survey Report* (Washington, D.C.), various issues.

research and development outlays increased in each year over this period. However, if one adjusts the research and development expenditures total for inflation, the result is very little growth in constant dollar research and development expenditures over the last four years of the period.[6] The GNP price deflator was used to convert current to real expenditures, and since this is

---

[6] In a recent paper, Caglarcan, Faust, and Schnee conclude that real research and development expenditures of the industry have remained constant since 1970. Their definition is similar to that employed in Table 3 except they exclude extramural research and development expenditures in the United States. See Erol Caglarcan, Richard Faust, and Jerome Schnee, "Resource Allocation in Pharmaceutical Research and Development" in Mitchell and Link, *Impact of Public Policy on Drug Innovation and Pricing*, pp. 332-337.

likely to have understated the rate of price change in research and development activity, the last few years in fact may have been characterized by negative growth rates in constant research and development dollars. Table 3 also shows that the research and development to sales ratio peaks in 1971.

In Table 3 the general time pattern of research and development expenditures for the drug industry is not atypical of the pattern that exists in other sectors. National Science Foundation data on total research and development expenditures for all industrial sectors also show declining research and development growth rates and decreasing research and development to sales ratios over recent periods. However, the growth rate in domestic research and development expenditures in the drug industry has been less than that for the entire industrial sector since 1971, whereas it was much higher for the earliest years in which the National Science Foundation obtained this data (the late 1950s and early 1960s).

The trends in pharmaceutical research and development allocations in recent years thus appear to be consistent with the idea that low rates of return to research and development have directed drug industry resources to alternative investment activities.[7] It remains to be seen, however, whether what has happened in the last few years will continue in future periods.

Shifts in Research and Development Activity Abroad

Since the drug industry is multinational in character, one obvious substitute for domestic research and development activity is foreign research and development. In Table 3, the time pattern of foreign research and development expenditures by U.S. drug firms is presented for the period 1961–1974. Foreign research and development expenditures have historically made up a relatively small proportion of total research and development expenditures. However, in the 1972–1974 period, as the growth rate in domestic research and development outlays declined markedly, foreign research and development expenditures by U.S. firms more than doubled. This rapid rate of growth in foreign research

---

[7] Dr. Lewis Sarett, president of Merck, Sharp & Dohme Research Laboratories, indicates a corresponding decline in the number of research projects being undertaken by the industry. Merck, in particular, has curtailed the number of research projects by 10 percent since 1969. See L. H. Sarett, "FDA Regulations and Their Influence on Future R and D," *Research Management*, vol. 27, no. 1 (March 1974), pp. 18-20.

and development expenditures by U.S. firms is also reflected in the percentage of total research and development accounted for by foreign activities. This increased from 9.9 percent in 1972 to 15.4 percent in 1974.

Lasagna and Wardell examine the general question of location of research and development activities in a paper presented to the 1974 AEI conference.[8] Their study is based on a questionnaire survey of the fifteen largest firms (firms that carry out 80 percent of the industry's research and development). These firms were asked to supply information on new chemical entities they had tested on humans since 1962. All fifteen firms responded to the questionnaire.

One of the questions asked concerned the location at which these U.S. firms first tested each new chemical entity introduced into man. Figure 3, depicting the percentage of total NCEs first studied abroad, shows some dramatic changes over time. Although the firms in the Lasagna-Wardell survey did almost no initial testing abroad before 1966, the percentage of NCEs first studied abroad grows rapidly after that point. By 1974, the last year of the sample, one-half of the NCEs were first tested abroad.[9]

Pharmaceutical research and development activity is also apparently growing at a much faster overall rate in other major developed countries than in the United States. Estimates of the rate of growth in pharmaceutical research and development expenditures and manpower for several developed countries over the period 1969–1972 are presented in Table 4. These were assembled by Harold Clymer from the sources given in this table.[10] They indicate that over this period the rate of growth in pharmaceutical research and development in each of these countries was more than double the rate for the United States. Moreover, as Clymer notes in his analysis of these data, these comparisons cannot be rationalized as simply reflecting a much lower base level of expenditures in these foreign countries. Total expenditures on pharmaceutical research and development for the European Economic Community member nations collectively now exceed those for the United States by a considerable margin. And Japan alone has annual research and development expenditures in

---

[8] Louis Lasagna and William M. Wardell, "The Rate of New Drug Discovery" in Helms, *Drug Development and Marketing*, pp. 155-164.

[9] Ibid., pp. 157-158.

[10] Harold Clymer, "The Economic and Regulatory Climate—U.S. and Overseas Trends" in Helms, *Drug Development and Marketing*, pp. 137-154.

Figure 3

LOCATION OF FIRST HUMAN STUDIES OF NCEs, 1963–1974

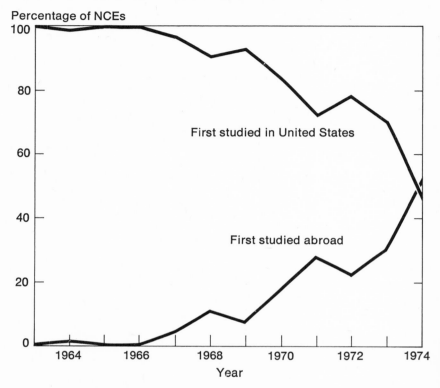

Source: Louis Lasagna, William M. Wardell, "The Rate of New Drug Discovery," in Robert B. Helms, ed., *Drug Development and Marketing* (Washington, D.C.: American Enterprise Institute for Public Policy Research, 1975), p. 157.

the pharmaceutical industry that are three-fourths of those for the United States.[11]

The data analyzed in this section clearly indicate (1) a strong tendency for U.S. firms to shift increasing percentages of their research and development abroad in recent years and (2) much faster overall growth rates in pharmaceutical industry research and development in foreign countries than in the United States. Whether these observed phenomena can be explained primarily by regulatory differences among countries, however, remains open to question. The main immediate output from research and devel-

---

[11] Ibid., p. 148.

Table 4

INTERNATIONAL GROWTH RATES IN PHARMACEUTICAL RESEARCH AND DEVELOPMENT, 1969–1972

(in percentages)

Countries	Estimated Annual Growth Rates	
	Expenditures	Manpower
United States	4-8	0-1
(West) Germany	15-20	8
United Kingdom	15-17	n.a.
Switzerland	25	n.a.
Sweden	14	8
Japan	22	15
France	15	8

Sources: Calculated by Harold Clymer from original sources. See Helms, *Drug Development and Marketing*, Table 7, p. 148.

opment activity is knowledge and information about the properties of a new drug. The developing firm normally appropriates this knowledge by establishing patent rights to its new drug in several countries. Even if the FDA should delay or prevent use of the patent rights on new chemical entities in the United States, it is not obvious that this by itself should cause firms to shift research and development abroad. In principle, knowledge about new drugs should be transferable to foreign subsidiaries so that the drugs could be introduced abroad. Moreover, the fact that the FDA has historically been less tolerant of foreign clinical data than foreign agencies have been of U.S. data should produce an economic incentive to keep research and development in this country.[12]

Nevertheless, there are factors at work in the opposite direction. Direct regulation of clinical research through the IND process has contributed to research and development costs higher in the United States than abroad. There may thus be substantial savings from carrying out research and development abroad even if the

---

[12] The FDA's announced intention to liberalize policies in this respect could produce an incentive in the opposite direction over future periods. (See, for example, Alexander Schmidt, "New Drugs for Investigational Use," *Federal Register* [Washington, D.C.: U.S. Government Printing Office, 1976], pp. 548-549.) It remains to be seen, however, what changes will actually occur concerning the FDA's policy on the acceptability of foreign data.

firms must subsequently duplicate all their clinical experiments in the United States. Firms could essentially "screen" new drug candidates abroad and conduct U.S. testing (with a lag) only on the successful drugs. In addition, firms have incentives to perform clinical trials in countries where the potential for new product sales is greatest in order to create a favorable climate for marketing acceptance by physicians and health officials in these countries. Evidence is presented in the next section showing that growth rates on new product sales in foreign countries have far exceeded those in the United States in recent years.

In sum, further investigation is necessary to determine the extent to which regulation is important in causing these shifts in research and development abroad as well as to determine the exact causal mechanism. Since research and development is an activity in which highly trained scientific and educated personnel are critical inputs, the availability and costs of such personnel also can be expected to influence these shifts. In addition, differences in the tax treatment of research and development and legal factors such as tort liability and patent protection may significantly influence location decisions.

Related International Developments

Harold Clymer has advanced a "regulatory-push demand-pull" hypothesis to explain shifts in research and development activity abroad. He views these transfers in research and development as the final step in a process of changing priorities and emphasis toward foreign markets by U.S. firms.[13] Specifically, he argues that

> An adverse micro-economic environment, resulting principally from the regulatory climate, seriously threatens the leadership of the domestic-based R&D activities of the technology intensive U.S. pharmaceutical industry. Their inability to grow in their home market through new product introductions and to obtain an adequate return on their R&D investment forces firms to give priority to foreign pharmaceutical markets, with eventual commensurate reallocation of their R&D resources, or to diversify into other business areas. In either case, the result is erosion of the extensive technological resources of the U.S. pharmaceutical industry.[14]

---

[13] Harold Clymer, "The Economic and Regulatory Climate: U.S. and Overseas Trends," pp. 137-154.
[14] Ibid., p. 139.

Clymer presents some international comparisons to support his central point that foreign markets are currently much more conducive to growth through new product introductions than is the U.S. market. He compares data on new product sales in the United States and United Kingdom over the five-year period 1968–1972. In each country he focuses on major products that achieved sales of at least $1 million. There were forty-four such products in the United Kingdom as against twenty-six in the United States in this five-year period. Clymer finds that the forty-four products introduced in the United Kingdom had a peak year sales volume comparable to that for the twenty-six products introduced in the United States ($220 million as against $240 million).[15] Thus, the U.K. market, which is only one-seventh the size of the total U.S. market, had sales volume for NCEs commensurate with that of the United States.

Clymer's analysis also indicates that the foreign sales of U.S. firms are currently growing at a much faster rate than their domestic sales. For example, over the period 1972 to 1973, he finds a 30 percent rate of growth in foreign sales for fifteen major pharmaceutical firms, while the rate of growth in domestic sales for these firms was only 10 percent. He predicts "with foreign sales increasing significantly more rapidly than U.S. sales, within the next five years, foreign markets will account for more than half of the U.S. pharmaceutical firms' total sales."[16]

Another development consistent with this shift in priorities by U.S. firms is the fact that the majority of NCE discoveries by U.S. firms are now first introduced abroad. This matter has been examined in the context of multi-country analysis by two German scientists, E. Reis-Arndt and D. Elvers (and later updated by Reis-Arndt).[17] In particular they investigate new chemical entity introductions on a worldwide basis for the period 1961–1973. They classify all NCEs according to both the country of origin and country of first introduction.[18] Their findings with respect to the

---

[15] Ibid., pp. 146-147.

[16] Ibid., p. 143.

[17] E. Reis-Arndt and D. Elvers, "Results of Pharmaceutical Research—New Pharmaceutical Agents 1961-1970" in *Drugs Made in Germany*, vol. 15, no. 3 (1972), pp. 134-140, and E. Reis-Arndt, "New Pharmaceutical Agents 1961-1973," *Drugs Made in Germany*, vol. 18, no. 3 (1975), pp. 123-130.

[18] In the case of multinational firms doing research and development outside their own country, the country of origin is assigned by Reis-Arndt and Elvers on the basis of the nationality of the parent firm rather than by the location of the initial research and development on the NCE. For a discussion, see E. Reis-Arndt, "New Pharmaceutical Agents," p. 123.

annual number of discoveries emanating from U.S. firms and the annual number of NCEs first introduced in the United States are shown in Table 5. This table also shows total annual NCEs introduced somewhere in the world (for the first time) for each year of the 1961–1973 period.

For the full thirteen-year period, the U.S. firms accounted for 24 percent of all NCEs introduced worldwide. However, the United States was the country of first introduction for only 9 percent of total NCEs. Furthermore, Table 5 shows that in the first few years of this period (1961–1962) the number of NCEs that were discovered by U.S. firms and the number of NCEs introduced first in the United States were reasonably comparable. After this

Table 5
WORLDWIDE NCE INTRODUCTIONS, 1961–1973, DISCOVERED BY U.S. FIRMS OR INSTITUTIONS OR FIRST INTRODUCED IN THE UNITED STATES

Year of First Introduction	Number of Annual First Introductions, Worldwide		
	Total	Discovered by U.S. firms or institutions	First introduced in U.S.
1961	91	31	26
1962	89	20	12
1963	96	22	7
1964	69	14	7
1965	73	13	4
1966	82	22	6
1967	85	20	5
1968	80	18	1
1969	76	18	3
1970	67	21	6
1971	82	25	6
1972	62	13	4
1973	65	10	5
Totals	1,017	247	92

Source: E. Reis-Arndt, "New Pharmaceutical Agents 1961–1973," in *Drugs Made in Germany*, vol. 18, p. 124.

time, however, the number of NCEs discovered by U.S. firms far exceeds the number first introduced in the United States. This indicates that after 1962 the vast majority of NCEs discovered by U.S. firms were first introduced abroad.

The introduction of NCEs abroad by U.S. firms before the drugs are introduced in the United States appears to be an institutional change strongly tied to differences in regulatory conditions. Among U.S. multinational firms such a research and marketing strategy is unique to the drug industry. The Reis-Arndt and Elvers analysis also indicates that a dramatic shift in firm behavior occurred between the pre- and post-amendment periods. This is consistent with the notion that regulatory differences between the United States and other countries after 1962 was a primary factor causing these shifts.

Regulatory differences have also apparently acted to accelerate drug firm investment in manufacturing capacity abroad. The tendency for multinational firms to substitute production abroad for exports is of course not unique to the drug industry, and for the drug industry it actually began before the 1962 amendments. The pattern is in fact predicted by foreign trade-cycle theory and is usually viewed as a defensive reaction by firms to protect overseas markets against foreign rivals.[19] Foreign tariff barriers and tax and licensing measures are among the factors that provide incentives to substitute foreign production for exports.

In the case of the drug industry, however, stringent regulatory conditions in the United States provide an additional inducement for firms to establish foreign manufacturing facilities, the more so because U.S. law prohibits the exporting of drugs not cleared by the FDA for marketing in the United States.[20] In order to minimize the "spillover" effects of increased U.S. regulatory constraints and delays on the introduction of NCEs in foreign markets, U.S. firms have a strong incentive to develop and expand foreign production and other foreign operations.

---

[19] See, for example, Raymond Vernon, *Sovereignty at Bay: The Multinational Spread of U.S. Enterprises* (New York: Basic Books, 1971).

[20] With regard to this point, the *Food Drug Cosmetic Law Reporter* states:

Drugs intended for export are not exempted from the new drug provisions of the [Federal Food, Drug, and Cosmetic] Act. A new drug may not be exported unless there is an effective new drug application for it, or unless it is shipped solely for investigational use to an expert.

[*Food Drug Cosmetic Law Reporter* (Commerce Clearing House: Chicago, 1975), ¶ 71,051, p. 71,054.]

In many ways, therefore, the tighter regulatory climate that has prevailed in the United States after 1962 has provided a strong incentive for U.S. firms to become more active in foreign markets. The last element in this movement of resources abroad involves the transfer of research and development activity to foreign countries. This phenomenon clearly has lagged other changes and has become evident only very recently. As I noted above, further research is clearly necessary to separate the role of regulation from other factors that might be causing these research and development shifts abroad.

The Clymer hypothesis, that these research and development shifts abroad are ultimately rooted in regulatory differences among countries and represent the final step in a historical transfer of priorities and resources to foreign countries offering greater growth opportunities, would certainly seem worthy of further analysis and attention. In principle, this hypothesis could be tested along with competing hypotheses by a formal statistical model like those discussed in the previous chapter.

Research Strategy

The changes that have occurred in the costs of and returns to developing new drugs in recent periods might be expected to cause changes in research and development strategy. To date, this is an area that has undergone no formal study. On the basis of his experiences, Dr. Lewis Sarett, president of Merck, Sharp, and Dohme Research Laboratories, has presented a number of hypotheses on what changes might be expected.[21] While we have touched on some of these points above (for example, overseas shifts in clinical pharmacology and related support), it will be useful to repeat some of his main hypotheses here. He postulates the following:

> *A relative shift of dollars from research to development.* There are few, if any, companies that can increase total R&D expenditures at the rate at which costs have escalated. More rapidly rising costs for development must thus result in a rising ratio of development to research. Three major companies showed a 15 to 25 percent shift of budget from research to development in 10 years.

---

[21] Lewis H. Sarett, "FDA Regulations and Their Influence on Future R & D," *Research Management,* vol. 17, no. 2 (March 1974), pp. 18-20.

A shift away from "me-too" drug research. . . . Research aimed at so-called "me-too" drugs has declined significantly and, in many therapeutic classes, essentially disappeared among the major drug houses in the last decade.

Increased emphasis on epidemiologically important diseases. With a reduction in total number of research projects, the survivors will tend to aim at the epidemiologically most important diseases. Those that occur more rarely will either be accorded nominal surveillance or—within economic limits—be supported through social responsibility of the industry.

Emphasis on total safety of drugs. An emphasis on complete and total freedom from risk, whether rationally achievable or not, has had its impact on research, quite apart from and in addition to its impact on development. The effort to avoid adverse drug reactions has led to new approaches to drug delivery systems with emphasis on release of the drug at the target organ, minimizing exposure of the rest of the body; unfortunately, such attempts may raise a whole new problem concerning the safety of the device or system itself, even when it accomplishes its purpose, and so on ad infinitum.

Increasing emphasis on research for drugs with short-term usage. Drugs for lifetime usage present problems in safety which are substantially greater than those used during acute illnesses. Accordingly, all aspects of preclinical and clinical studies tend to be prolonged with an attendant increase in costs and time. Hence, research programs in some companies will focus on drugs intended for acute and limited conditions.[22]

Two clear themes emerge from these hypotheses. One is that firms will attempt to offset the higher costs of drug development by concentrating on projects that will produce the largest market sales. This is reflected in the shift toward important disease areas and away from "me-too" research. At the same time Dr. Sarett postulates that all firms will also exhibit greater risk avoidance, given the greater riskiness that currently characterizes drug development. Thus, he suggests, firms will shift away from research toward development and toward drugs with short-term usage as well as increasingly attempt to develop drugs with targeted effects and minimal adverse impact.

---

[22] Ibid., pp. 19-20.

This twin emphasis on market potential and avoidance of risk has somewhat opposing effects on the nature of the drugs likely to emerge at the end of the research and development pipeline. This may explain in part why the average market shares of NCEs have not increased in recent periods, whereas one might have expected greater market shares to be captured by the fewer NCEs now being introduced.

In any case, Dr. Sarett has provided a number of provocative hypotheses on the way external changes in the environment are likely to change firm behavior and research and development strategy. Further analysis is clearly warranted to investigate the validity of these hypotheses and the magnitude of these and other changes that may be occurring in this area.

Summary and Conclusions

Research and development activity in the pharmaceutical industry has undergone significant changes in recent years. The analytical studies of the rate of return on domestic research and development indicate a declining rate of return over time and a consequent weakening of the incentives for private investment in innovational activity. There have been several further developments consistent with this finding. First, the rapid rate of growth in domestic research and development expenditures by the drug industry that characterized the 1950s and early 1960s has now ceased. In real terms the present rate of growth may even be negative. Second, U.S. firms are beginning to perform an increasing percentage of their research and development abroad. Third, significant changes appear to be occurring in the way firms allocate their research and development budgets among various projects.

None of these studies has attempted to make formal tests of hypotheses about the causal factors underlying these developments. Nevertheless, the overall pattern of results appears quite consistent with the findings discussed in the last chapter concerning the impact of regulation on innovation.

CHAPTER IV

STRUCTURAL EFFECTS OF REGULATION IN THE ETHICAL DRUG INDUSTRY

This chapter examines various structural effects of regulation. The first question considered is whether increased regulatory control has contributed to concentrating innovation in the largest firms in the ethical drug industry. The chapter then considers a number of related questions, including the effects of regulation on market concentration and on ethical drug prices.

Innovation and Firm Size

The general question of the relation of innovation to firm size has been the subject of considerable empirical study by economists interested in the process of technological change. A number of a priori theoretical arguments dating back to Schumpeter have been advanced as to why innovation might be concentrated in the larger firms in an industry.[1] These include the argument that the innovational process is risky, costly, and subject to economies of scale. On the other hand, critics of the Schumpeterian hypothesis have offered various counter-arguments why innovation will not be disproportionately concentrated in very large firms, among them that large firms may be more averse to risk than smaller firms and may also be subject to organizational diseconomies.[2]

For the drug industry, the initial empirical studies of this question were performed on separate cross-sectional data samples

---

[1] A good discussion of this issue is provided in F. M. Scherer, *Industrial Market Structure and Economic Performance* (Chicago: Rand McNally & Co., 1970), Chapter 15.

[2] See the discussion in Scherer, *Industrial Market Structure*, pp. 352-354.

over the late 1950s and early 1960s. Studies by Mansfield, Comanor, Grabowski, and Schnee used different output and input indices of innovational activity and worked with samples ranging from a dozen or so firms to much larger aggregations (over fifty firms).[3] These studies found no tendency for innovational activity to be disproportionately concentrated in the largest drug firms.

The structural changes associated with the 1962 amendments might be expected, however, to cause firm size to assume a more important role in the innovational process than was previously the case. The regulatory changes increased both cost and risk in the development process. In particular, the proof of efficacy requirement and the IND review increase the number of tests and the costs of development. Given more stringent regulatory criteria on safety and efficacy, the probability of FDA approval is also lowered for many compounds. While the effects on expected profits from higher costs and lower probability of approval might be offset in part or whole by higher profit margins and longer product lives for NCEs (with fewer new drugs being approved for marketing), the returns to drug development tend to be more variable and hence subject to greater risk. Presumably, large firms are better able to bear these higher costs and diversify the risk by carrying a large portfolio of research projects.

Because of these developments, one might expect to observe a stronger relation between firm size and innovation in the post-1962 period than before the amendment. In a recent paper, John Vernon and I perform an extensive analysis of this question.[4] In particular, we examine the relation of innovation to firm size using the same cross-section of firms and the same structural models for the pre- and post-amendment periods. We also investigate comparable structural changes for the U.K. drug industry.

Some summary findings from our study are presented in Table 6. Information is shown there on the number of firms producing new chemical entities as well as the concentration of innovation in the largest firms (ranked by sales). Innovational

---

[3] Mansfield, *Industrial Research and Technological Innovation*, pp. 38-42; W. S. Comanor, "Research and Technical Change in the Pharmaceutical Industry," *Review of Economics and Statistics*, vol. 47, no. 2 (May 1965), pp. 182-190; Henry Grabowski, "The Determinants of Industrial Research and Development: A Study of the Chemical, Drug, and Petroleum Industries," *Journal of Political Economy*, vol. 76, no. 2 (March-April 1968), pp. 292-305; Jerome E. Schnee, "Innovation and Discovery in the Ethical Pharmaceutical Industry" in Edwin Mansfield et al., *Research and Innovation in the Modern Corporation* (New York: W. W. Norton, 1971), pp. 157-185.

[4] Grabowski and Vernon, "Structural Effects of Regulation," *passim*.

Table 6

STRUCTURAL SHIFTS IN THE RELATION OF INNOVATION TO FIRM SIZE FOR U.S. AND U.K. PHARMACEUTICAL INDUSTRY

Period	Total NCEs (1)	Share of NCE Sales to Total Sales (2)	Number of Firms with an NCE (3)	Largest Four Firms: Share of innovation (4)	Share of sales (5)	Ratio (6)
United States:						
1957–61	233	20.0	51	24.0	26.5	0.91
1962–66	93	8.6	34	25.0	24.0	1.04
1967–71	76	5.5	23	48.7	26.1	1.87
United Kingdom:						
1962–66	115	13.3	48	39.9	26.9	1.48
1967–71	95	12.9	44	14.5	29.5	0.49

Note: Column (1)—NCEs in this table are defined identically for the United States and the United Kingdom. However, NCEs used exclusively or primarily in hospitals are excluded for the United Kingdom since only drugstore sales information was available. See also note (a) of Table 1 and the text for further details. Column (2)—Average annual sales of all NCEs introduced during this period as a percentage of total ethical drug sales in last year of the period. Column (3)—Self-explanatory. Column (4)—Percentage of innovational output accounted for by four largest firms (ranked by ethical drug sales) where innovational output is measured as total new chemical entity sales during first three years after introduction. Column (5)—Percentage of total ethical drug sales accounted for by four largest firms. Column (6)—Ratio of share of innovation (column 4) to share of sales (column 5).

Sources: U.S. data—new chemical entities in each year obtained from Paul de Haen, *Annual New Products Parade,* various issues; all data on ethical drug sales obtained from Intercontinental Medical Statistics, Ltd. See Table 10-1 in Henry Grabowski and John Vernon, "Structural Effects of Regulation in the Drug Industry," forthcoming in Robert Masson, editor, *Essays on Industrial Organization in Honor of Joe Bain* (Cambridge, Mass.: Ballinger, 1976), p. 192. U.K. data—list of new chemical entities in each year obtained from Paul de Haen, *Nonproprietary Name Index,* and special reports by de Haen. All data on sales obtained from Intercontinental Medical Statistics, Ltd. See Table 10-6 in Grabowski and Vernon, "Structural Effects of Regulation in the Drug Industry," p. 200.

output is measured as the total sales of new chemical entities for each firm during the first three full years of product life for the NCEs. In Table 6, the data on trends in the United States are broken into three subperiods: the pre-amendment time interval (1957–1961) and two five-year intervals in the post-amendment periods (1962–1966 and 1967–1971). Splitting the post-amendment period in this fashion has a number of advantages. First there is some evidence that the impacts of the 1962 amendments did not all occur in 1962, but were distributed over time; in particular, average regulatory clearance times have exhibited an upward time trend since 1962.[5] Second, structural relations like those analyzed here would not be expected to change instantaneously with a shift in regulatory climate. Rather, because they are cumulative in nature, they would change only gradually over time. Five-year subperiods also provide intervals in the post-amendment period to the comparable five-year interval with available data from the pre-amendment period.

The first two columns in Table 6 show the decline that took place in the number and sales of new chemical entities in the United States in the post-amendment period. These data have previously been discussed in Chapter II. Column (3) shows that the number of firms introducing NCEs has also declined significantly, with the number of firms introducing NCEs in the 1967–1971 period less than half the number introducing NCEs in the 1957–1961 period. Columns (4) and (5) show trends in the percentage of innovational output (as defined above) and overall market shares of the four largest firms. In the final subperiod a dramatic shift occurs with the four largest U.S. firms accounting for a much larger share of innovation (48.7) than of total ethical drug sales (26.1). This datum, of course, provides only one index for determining whether innovation is becoming disproportionately concentrated in the largest firms. Further analysis in our paper (involving quadratic and cubic regressions as well as trends in concentration measures of innovational output so defined) show similar dramatic changes occurring over recent time periods. Our results clearly show not only that the rate of innovation has significantly declined in the post-amendment period, but that it also has become concentrated in fewer and larger firms.

In order to gain a further perspective on the role of regulation in producing these structural changes, we also examine comparable structural developments in the United Kingdom. The data currently available in the United Kingdom are much more limited in character than those available in the United States. We were

---

[5] Some evidence for this proposition is provided by Lasagna and Wardell, "The Rate of New Drug Discovery" in Helms, ed., *Drug Development and Marketing*, pp. 155-181. See also J. M. Jadlow, "The Economic Effects of the 1962 Amendments" (Ph.D. diss., University of Virginia, 1970), p. 174.

able to obtain information on new product introductions and sales only over the period (1962–1974) corresponding to the U.S. post-amendment period. Moreover, these sales data are confined to drugstores and exclude hospital purchases. For this reason drugs used exclusively or primarily in hospitals (injections, for example) are excluded from the analysis. Some drugs with low or zero sales are not included because data were unavailable. However, because we are primarily interested in determining directional shifts in structural relations and variables over time, these limitations should not significantly bias our results.

In the lower half of Table 6, statistics comparable to those on the United States are presented for the United Kingdom over the subperiods 1962–1966 and 1967–1971. These data indicate that in the United Kingdom NCE sales maintained a much higher share of total ethical drug sales (column 2) than they did in the United States.[6] Column (3) further shows that the number of firms producing at least one NCE remained relatively stable over these two periods. Finally, columns (4) and (5) show that the innovational share of the four largest firms relative to their share of sales declined sharply from the first period to the second [from 1.48 in 1962–1966 to 0.49 in 1967–1971, as can be seen in column (6)].

Table 6 shows that the United States and United Kingdom have been characterized by very different structural trends in the period after 1962. It is therefore difficult to attribute the developments in each country to a common underlying causal factor (for example, a depletion of scientific opportunities making research and development costlier and riskier). Instead, a more plausible interpretation of these findings is that the more stringent post-1962 regulatory climate in the United States led to a stronger tie between innovation and large firm size in the United States. This interpretation also receives some support from our findings regarding the performance of U.S. firms in the United Kingdom in the post-1962 period. This topic is discussed in the section immediately following.

---

[6] It should be noted that a computational error which inflated the values reported for the U.K. share measure in an earlier paper (Grabowski and Vernon, "Structural Effects of Regulation," Table 10-6) has been corrected here. Some tendency for these numbers to *understate* the true values in the United Kingdom necessarily remains, however, because of the data omissions discussed in the previous paragraph and the note to Table 6.

The Post-1962 Performance of U.S. Firms in the United Kingdom and the "Echo Effect" of Regulation

Another interesting finding that emerges from our study concerns the performance of U.S. firms in the U.K. ethical drug market after 1962. Specifically, the share of U.K. ethical drug sales accounted for by U.S. firms decreased significantly over the period from 1962 to 1973. In 1962, U.S. firms had a total market share of 46.9 percent of U.K. ethical drug sales, whereas by 1973 their share had declined to 38.4 percent. Only over the last few years of this period is there any tendency for this downward trend to bottom out and turn around.[7]

An even more dramatic decline is observed in the U.S. firms' share of new drug product innovation over the period 1962–1972. U.S. firms and their subsidiaries accounted for 54 percent of total new product innovation [as measured in column (4) of Table 6] in the United Kingdom over the period 1961–1966 and only 15 percent in 1967–1971. This sharp decline in the innovative performance by U.S. firms in the latter period helps explain why innovational output became much less concentrated in the United Kingdom over these two periods of time [column (6) of Table 5].

The declining share of U.K. new product innovation and total drug sales accounted for by U.S. firms in the post-1962 period might be plausibly explained as a lagged response or "echo" effect to the tighter regulatory climate that took effect in the United States in the early 1960s. Before the 1962 amendments, the prevalent strategy of U.S. firms apparently was to introduce their products first into the U.S. market and then introduce them (with a lag) into foreign countries. Moreover, these new products were often manufactured here and exported abroad in the earlier stages of their product life cycle. However, as the U.S. regulatory environment became more stringent and the number of NCEs cleared in the United States declined sharply, the stock of U.S. new product innovations available for subsequent introduction abroad also declined. Hence, one might expect that a corresponding decline would take place (somewhat lagged in time) in the innovational performance of U.S. firms abroad. This is precisely what is observed in the United Kingdom over the decade 1962–1971.

---

[7] Grabowski and Vernon, "Structural Effects of Regulation," Table 10-10, pp. 202-203.

As was discussed in the last chapter, U.S. firms have also changed many of their strategies and institutional practices over this period to allow for better exploitation of the faster growing foreign markets. By the early 1970s, U.S. firms had extensive operations in the United Kingdom and elsewhere and were introducing drugs in foreign countries without reference to U.S. regulatory decisions. In addition, by this time the last element in this shift of priorities and resources abroad—the performance of research and development activities in foreign countries—had also begun to occur to a significant degree.

As a consequence of these large shifts in technical and physical resources by U.S. firms abroad, the future performance of U.S. firms in foreign countries may not duplicate their immediate post-1962 experience. Indeed, the fact that growth in foreign sales for U.S. firms in the last few years has been much greater than their domestic sales suggests that the impact of these shifts in resources and priorities abroad are already being felt.

These developments would seem to raise some important questions for further work. They suggest the possibility that innovational activity in the ethical drug industry in the future might increasingly be dominated not merely by relatively large firms (as our results above indicate) but also by firms that have an extensive multinational orientation and character. It is the latter type of firm that would appear to be in the best position to shift resources on a worldwide basis in order to avoid some of the costs of the more stringent regulatory environment in this country. Certainly, this is a question that has a high priority for future research.

Trends in Market Concentration

Given that new product innovation has become more concentrated in larger firms over recent years, it is interesting to consider whether similar increases have occurred in the concentration of the ethical drug sales.

In our forthcoming study, John Vernon and I examine recent trends in market sales concentration for both the U.S. and the U.K. ethical drug industries. We find a distinct upward trend in market concentration in the United States over recent years, though so far it has been quite modest in size. Between 1962 and 1973, for example, the four-firm concentration ratio of sales increased from 25.4 percent to 27.8 percent. Over the same period market concentration in the United Kingdom declined but the changes there were also modest in kind.[8]

An interesting question that follows from these findings is why market concentration has changed only slightly in each country while the concentration of innovational activity has changed significantly. The disparity could reflect a number of factors. One is the matter of time lags. That is, increasing concentration in innovation may influence total market sales only with significant time lags and have a slow cumulative impact over time. An analysis of our U.S. data indicates that the effect of new product innovation on market shares builds to a peak somewhere between five and ten years after introduction.[9] Since the observed increase in concentration of innovation among the largest firms was pronounced only in the last five-year period (1967–1971) in Table 6, it is evident that the full effects of these changes on market concentration may not become apparent for some time.

It should also be noted that some of the recent developments in the U.S. ethical drug market may operate to produce less rather than more concentration in market sales over the long run. As discussed above, the percentage of total ethical drug sales accounted for by new products has declined significantly over time [column (2) of Table 6]. Thus a substantially greater portion of drugs being sold are "old" drugs and new product innovation has declined as a competitive factor in the industry. In addition, increases in new product development and regulatory approval time have worked to shorten the effective patent lives of new drugs.[10] Reduced levels of new product innovation and shorter patent lives are factors leading, over the long term, to an equilibrium position in which fewer drugs would be subject to patent protection. This is likely to have deconcentrating rather than concentrating effects on ethical drug sales.

In sum, although increasing concentration of innovational activity may be expected to produce similar tendencies in market concentration, it is difficult to predict the net effect on market concentration of all the developments currently taking place in the ethical drug industry. Furthermore, since most of these factors influence market concentration only with significant time lags, it may be some time before one can discern predominant influences.

---

[8] Ibid., pp. 195 and 202.

[9] Ibid., p. 196.

[10] Some evidence on effective patent lives is provided in David Schwartzman, *Innovation in the Pharmaceutical Industry* (Baltimore: Johns Hopkins University Press, forthcoming).

Market Competition and Drug Prices

The decline in the supply of new chemical entities means a decline in competition for existing drugs. Other things equal, one would expect this to result in higher prices for existing drugs.

Sam Peltzman has investigated the short-run implications of a diminished supply of new chemical entities on the prices of established drugs.[11] Using a simple regression equation, he estimates that for each decrease of 1 percent in market share of NCEs there is a corresponding 0.13 percent increase in drug prices. He interprets this increase as resulting from the diminished competition from new drugs. Although this appears to be a relatively moderate effect, Peltzman estimates a cost of approximately $50 million annually to consumers of drugs.

The two-variable regression model used by Peltzman only provides a first-level analysis of this question.[12] Nevertheless, his findings are consistent with theoretical expectations.

Summary and Conclusions

An analysis of various structural changes in the U.S. ethical drug industry indicates that innovation has become increasingly concentrated over time in the larger firms and that the number of independent sources for new drug discoveries and introductions has declined. A comparative analysis of the U.K. industry shows that comparable changes in innovative concentration have not been experienced there. Innovation in the United Kingdom became less rather than more concentrated in the largest-sized firms over the post-1962 period. This declining trend in innovational concentration in the United Kingdom is apparently due in considerable part to a sharply declining rate of innovation by U.S. firms in the United Kingdom in that period.

These developments, together with those discussed in the previous chapters, appear related to (or symptomatic of) fundamental underlying changes in the innovational process. While several factors may be relevant here, the results from international comparative analyses particularly suggest that increased U.S. regulation has had a significant independent effect on the structural changes occurring in the United States.

---

[11] Peltzman, "Benefits and Costs," pp. 170-172.

[12] See Telser's critique of Peltzman's study in Landau, *Regulating New Drugs*, p. 217.

CHAPTER V

COST/BENEFIT ANALYSES OF THE 1962 AMENDMENTS

The empirical work discussed so far is in the domain of positive rather than normative economics. That is, it attempts to estimate what the effects of the 1962 regulatory changes have been rather than say what policy changes are desirable or what an ideal regulatory policy would be. A few studies have attempted to move beyond positive analyses to normative evaluations of the amendments, using the framework of a cost-benefit analysis. Because the original legislation was designed as a consumer-protection measure, these analyses have been set up to assess whether consumers on balance have been made better or worse off by the 1962 amendments.

James Jondrow's Cost-Benefit Analysis

The first cost-benefit analysis of the 1962 amendments was performed by James Jondrow in a Ph.D. dissertation at the University of Wisconsin.[1] He concludes that the benefit-cost ratio of the amendments for consumers is highly favorable. The benefits in Jondrow's models are the estimated decrease in sales of "ineffective" drugs in the post-amendment period. Ratings of drug efficacy are obtained from the National Academy of Science efficacy review undertaken for the FDA for all active drugs introduced before 1962. The cost to consumers in his model is that portion of increased research and development expenditures resulting from

---

[1] James M. Jondrow, "A Measure of the Monetary Benefits and Costs to Consumers of the Regulation of Prescription Drug Effectiveness" (Ph.D. diss., University of Wisconsin, 1972).

the amendments that is passed on to consumers in the form of higher prices for new drugs. Jondrow estimates a benefit-cost ratio of 2.24, assuming that *all* estimated increased research and development costs are passed on to consumers. Since this assumption tends to overestimate price increases borne by consumers, Jondrow argues that his benefit-cost ratio is conservative and understates the true value of the amendments to consumers. Moreover, from an overall social perspective, he estimates that benefits exceed costs by more than a two-to-one margin.

Jondrow's model does not impute any costs from the amendments in the form of a reduced supply of "effective" drugs. He implicitly assumes that the large decline in total NCEs in the post-amendment period either (1) was caused by factors other than the 1962 regulations, or (2) represented drugs that would have duplicated existing drugs in therapeutic benefits and therefore would not have yielded any net gains in consumer surplus. Since a number of the empirical studies discussed above point to different conclusions on both these points, Jondrow's analysis is defective in its omission of this indirect but nevertheless potentially significant cost of the amendments to the consumers.

Furthermore, the National Academy of Science efficacy review (which Jondrow used to determine drug efficacy) considered only whether sufficient evidence existed for pre-1962 drug efficacy, not whether the drugs involved were actually effective. Subsequent studies have, for a number of the "ineffective" drugs, provided evidence of efficacy that is satisfactory by modern standards. Thus, by this approach Jondrow overestimates the benefits of the amendments.

Sam Peltzman's Study

A more comprehensive and widely cited cost-benefit analysis of the 1962 amendments was performed by Sam Peltzman.[2] His conclusions are quite different from Jondrow's. He finds that the costs of the amendments to consumers far exceed the benefits. He uses as basic inputs in the cost-benefit analysis his estimates of the effects of the amendments on the decline in NCEs discussed in Chapter II.

Like Jondrow, Peltzman assumes that the benefits to consumers from the amendments accrue from the reduction in ineffec-

---

[2] Peltzman, *Regulation of Pharmaceutical Innovation,* and Peltzman, "Costs and Benefits," pp. 19-48.

tive drugs. Although both scholars find comparable rates of ineffective drug usage in the pre-amendment period, they value the benefits in different ways, and Peltzman obtains a somewhat lower estimate of annual benefits. At the same time, Peltzman estimates that the largest component of the cost to consumers arises from the reduced flow of effective new drugs caused by the amendments. This component is completely ignored in Jondrow's analysis. Finally, the models are apparently in accord in their findings that there are positive costs to consumers arising from higher prices of new drugs but that these are relatively small in magnitude.

The main difference between the two studies is thus the large imputed costs to the amendments from the decline in effective NCEs, included in Peltzman's analysis but omitted in Jondrow's. This imputed cost component in turn depends critically on estimates of (1) the degree to which the decline in NCEs is attributable specifically to the amendments and (2) the value of this foregone flow of NCEs to consumers. Since the first question has already been discussed at length in Chapter II, I shall focus my present discussion on the second.

Peltzman uses a consumer-surplus methodology to calculate gains and losses from the amendments. In particular, he estimates a demand schedule for new drugs from data on drug output and prices (aggregated by therapeutic class) in the pre- and post-amendment periods. He then uses this schedule to estimate shifts in consumer surplus under the two regulatory regimes.

Peltzman's means of estimating costs to consumers from the reduced supply of new drugs can be illustrated by reference to a diagram like that in Figure 4. Consider two states of the world (the pre- and post-amendment states) and also assume a price *B* per unit exists in both periods. Demand curve *ADM* corresponds to the level of demand in the pre-amendment state of the world. Demand curve *GHEN*, which is below and to the left of *ADM*, corresponds to demand in the post-amendment state. The post-amendment curve is below the pre-amendment curve essentially for two reasons. First, certain drugs that could be classed as effective are no longer available or no longer marketed because of the amendments, and demand for these drugs is consequently nonexistent. Second, some of the drugs that do become available are officially restricted to the therapeutic uses for which the FDA deems them effective. Restrictions of this sort can result in a loss of consumer welfare if the FDA fails to approve a drug for all areas in which it is effective. The decline in demand given in Figure 4 leads to a post-amendment loss in consumer welfare equal to the area *GHDA*. It is this area that Peltzman estimates using empirical demand schedules for new drugs in the pre- and post-amendment periods.

Peltzman's estimates of benefits to consumers from the amendments can also be illustrated from a diagrammatic analysis like that of Figure 4. Assume that in the pre-amendment period drugs are marketed that are not effective for some or all of the uses claimed in their advertisements. Peltzman assumes demand for such drugs will initially be inflated. Over time, however, as consumers learn from experience, demand schedules for these

Figure 4

DEMAND CURVES FOR NEW DRUGS

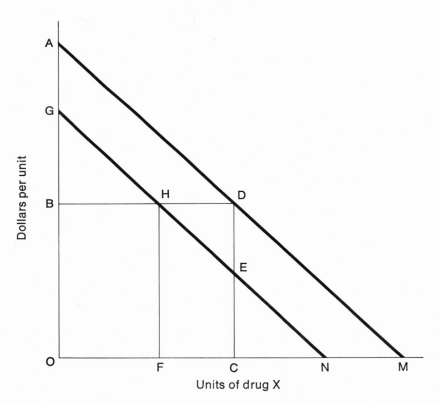

Source: See Peltzman, *Regulation of Pharmaceutical Innovation*, p. 24.

drugs will shift downward. If we assume that demand curve *ADM* represents the inflated pre-consumer learning demand curve and demand curve *GHEN* is the true after-consumer learning curve, there is a loss in consumer welfare equal to *HDE* from consumer misinformation in the pre-amendment situation. It is this triangular loss of welfare that Peltzman assumes will be eliminated by the FDA screens for efficacy in the post-amendment period. Estimates of this pre-amendment loss to consumers depend critically on what portion of the pre-amendment NCEs are ineffective and how fast the consumer-learning process takes place. These data are estimated by Peltzman from growth rate patterns over time in the pre- and post-amendment periods (as discussed in Chapter II above).

On the basis of this analysis, Peltzman presents the following summary of his main results:

> Treated as a group, consumers seem clearly to have lost on balance from the amendments. Their annual gains and losses break down as follows: (1) missed benefits (consumer surplus from the reduced flow of new drugs), producing a loss of \$300–400 million; (2) reduced waste on purchases of ineffective new drugs, producing a gain of under \$100 million; and (3) higher prices for existing drugs because of reduced competition from new drugs, producing a loss of \$50 million. These measurable effects add up to a net loss of \$250 to \$350 million, or about 6 percent of total drug sales.[3]

He then draws the following policy conclusions:

> If the Food, Drug and Cosmetic Act was intended to benefit consumers, the inescapable conclusion to which this study points is that the intent is better served by reversion to the status quo ante 1962. This conclusion follows directly from the size of the problem with which the 1962 amendments sought to cope. Consumer losses from purchases of ineffective drugs or hastily marketed unsafe drugs appear to have been trivial compared to gains from innovation. In this context, any perceptible deterrent to innovation was bound to impose net losses on consumers. The amendments clearly provided such a deterrent.[4]

---

[3] Peltzman, *Regulation of Pharmaceutical Innovation*, p. 81.
[4] Ibid., p. 82.

Although Peltzman's analysis is clearly insightful, his policy conclusions are subject to a number of qualifications. In the discussion following here, I first consider some technical qualifications to Peltzman's analysis, and then discuss the nature of policy conclusions that can be drawn from an aggregate cost-benefit analysis of this type.

As we noted above, a critical input in any cost-benefit analysis of the amendments is the effect of the amendments (as compared to the effect of other factors) in causing the sharp decline in NCEs in the post-amendment period. On the basis of the demand-pull model discussed in Chapter II, Peltzman concludes that all the reduced flow in NCEs results from changes in FDA regulation. However, as I pointed out in that chapter, his model does not formally include any supply-side factors relating to the depletion of scientific knowledge. At best, these factors might be imperfectly captured in his model by the lagged cumulative value of past NCE introductions (a variable which is included in his analysis for other reasons).

Peltzman employs a residual analysis to estimate the effects of regulation on the supply of NCEs, and it is likely that his estimated residual includes the effects of other factors (such as the depletion of knowledge) that operate contemporaneously with regulation but are not explicitly accounted for by proxy variables. The international comparative studies reviewed in Chapter II seem to suggest that other factors besides regulation may have negatively influenced the level of NCE introductions here and abroad in the post-amendment period. Peltzman's analysis, which allocates all the reduction in the flow of NCEs to the amendments, is therefore subject to an upward bias of unknown magnitude in its estimate of the cost to consumers. Further investigation would seem warranted to determine the importance of this upward bias.

A different set of issues concerns Peltzman's use of consumer-surplus methodology to estimate the value of gains or losses to consumers from the reduced flow of NCEs. Although this is a standard approach in cost-benefit analysis, its applicability has been questioned for markets like ethical drugs where consumers have a limited role in selecting the final products consumed. Specifically, it has been argued that doctors will be much less price-sensitive than patients. In addition, many drugs are paid for through third-party payment schemes, and this can also serve to distort the drug valuation imputed from estimated market demand curves. These factors influence Peltzman's measure of benefits and costs in a qualitatively similar fashion, which means that they may not change the final outcome. They do, however, introduce uncertainties about his calculated values of benefits and costs.

At a less fundamental level, Thomas McGuire, Richard Nelson, and Thomas Spavins have pointed out some other technical problems relating to Peltzman's methodology in calculating benefits and costs.[5] I shall not discuss their critique in any detail here, but it should be noted that their main thrust is directed at the use of shifts in *aggregate* demand curves to deduce how *individual consumers* learn and respond to uncertainties about drug efficacy. They argue that uncertainty about a new drug's efficacy will not necessarily produce uniform behavior on the part of consumers. For example, in a less stringent regulatory environment where the FDA did not review drug efficacy claims, some doctors might err on the side of caution and initially underprescribe rather than overprescribe new drugs. The curves of some consumers (doctors, patients) in the pre-amendment period may thus behave in a fashion opposite to what is assumed in Figure 4. If this is the case, shifts in aggregate demand curves for new drugs may not be a good indicator of the learning experiences of individual consumers. Peltzman appears to accept these criticisms in principle, but argues that from an operational standpoint it does not tend to bias his central finding—that the costs of the amendments far exceeded the benefits.[6]

It is my own opinion that questions of valuation, while important, are less critical to the final conclusions than questions of the cause and nature of the decline in innovation in the post-amendment period. If the basic results which Peltzman uses as inputs to his cost-benefit analysis hold up—namely (1) that the vast majority of new drugs introduced in the pre-amendment period were effective and (2) that the amendments caused the drug innovation rate to be more than halved and the gestation period to be more than doubled—then his basic conclusion that the costs substantially outweigh the benefits would probably hold under any alternative scheme of assigning values to these outcomes.

[5] Thomas McGuire, Richard Nelson, and Thomas Spavins, "An Evaluation of Consumer Protection Legislation: The 1962 Drug Amendments: A Comment," *Journal of Political Economy,* vol. 83, no. 3 (May-June 1975), pp. 655-662.

[6] Sam Peltzman, "An Evaluation of Consumer Protection Legislation: The 1962 Drug Amendments: A Reply," *Journal of Political Economy,* vol. 83, no. 3 (May-June 1975), pp. 663-668.

Apart from technical qualifications, the policy implications of Peltzman's work are limited by the aggregative nature of his analysis. Because a dummy-variable procedure is used to capture regulatory differences in the pre- and post-amendment periods, the analysis cannot distinguish the separate effects of particular changes in regulatory standards or conditions. Rather, at best, it can measure the net impact of all the changes that occurred. Moreover, many of these changes might have taken place independent of any legislative changes. Peltzman's wording of his policy conclusions seems implicitly to recognize this when he says that his analysis implies that consumers would be better off by "a reversion to the status quo ante 1962." A reversion to the status quo ante 1962 in this case, however, would mean not only a repeal of all the formal requirements of the 1962 amendments, but also a reversion from all other changes in the regulatory climate that took place after 1962. This would include changes in the attitudes of regulators, organizational procedures, and so on.

The FDA obviously had considerable discretionary authority before the amendments. It would not be unreasonable to argue that, given the wide publicity and emotional impact of the thalidomide incident, the regulatory process would have grown more stringent after 1962 regardless of any congressional actions. Changes in the post-1962 situation might be significantly related to shifts in regulatory conditions, but these shifts would encompass more than the formal changes concerning proof of efficacy and other requirements of the 1962 amendments. Furthermore, any repeal of the amendments not accompanied by corresponding changes in regulatory attitudes and incentives might only partially reduce the costs attributed to the amendments.

Both Peltzman and Jondrow give primary analytical attention to the changes resulting from the proof of efficacy requirement. However, this was only one of the major legal changes produced by the amendments. They also included the requirement that research protocols on clinical testing be submitted and subject to FDA approval (the IND process). In accordance with this new responsibility, the FDA set forth fairly specific (and continuously increasing) standards for the animal toxicology studies necessary before any testing on humans is allowed. The process of drug discovery and development therefore came under direct regulatory control and scrutiny for the first time. On a priori grounds, this could be expected to lead to a significant increase in research and development costs and contribute to a lessened rate of new product innovation. At the same time it is a source of potential benefits to volunteers and patients in the form of greater protection in the experimental testing process.

In many ways, the IND requirement represented a much sharper break with the pre-1962 environment than the proof-of-efficacy standard. As Professors Wardell and Lasagna note, some attention was paid to efficacy before 1962 under the FDA's mandate to insure safety.[7] They argue that because no drug is absolutely safe, the decision whether a drug is safe enough to be licensed must depend on the use to which it is put and hence its efficacy. This kind of procedure—evaluating a drug's benefits relative to its risks—governed FDA decisions before and after 1962. In the years since it obtained a formal mandate to insure efficacy, the FDA has apparently instituted much tighter standards on efficacy than it had applied before. Hence firms have been required to devote much greater resources to demonstrating efficacy than they devoted previously. However, this represents more a quantitative than a qualitative change in regulatory procedures.

International comparative analyses show that identical regulations may be implemented in quite different ways, and this in turn can produce very different outcomes. Sir Derrick Dunlop, in his analysis of U.S. and U.K. systems, emphasizes that differences in organizational structures and incentives are as important as (or more important than) differences in formal regulations in explaining the regulatory behavior in the two countries since 1962.[8] An aggregate cost-benefit analysis picks up the net impact of all the changes in regulatory conditions, formal and informal, that have occurred since 1962. Hence, it is difficult to predict from such an analysis which particular policy changes would have the highest payoffs.

Peltzman's analysis provides evidence to support the position that the aggregate costs of the more stringent regulatory conditions after 1962 have exceeded the aggregate benefits. His analysis indicates the dominant element in the cost to consumers has been the reduced rate of new product innovation in the post-1962 period. If it is assumed that the technical qualifications discussed above can be overcome, the key remaining question for public policy is what specific changes could be undertaken to reduce the significant adverse side effects of regulation on drug innovation.

---

[7] Wardell and Lasagna, *Regulation and Drug Development*, p. 16.

[8] Dunlop, "British System of Drug Regulation," pp. 234-237.

In order to answer this question, further microeconomic analysis would seem necessary to complement the aggregative approach carried out by Peltzman.

While there are a number of problems for further work, Peltzman's cost-benefit analysis represents an important first step in gaining some perspective on the overall costs and benefits of increased regulatory controls. It provides a serious challenge to the conventional wisdom that assumes governmental regulation will lead to increases in consumer welfare.

CHAPTER VI

POLICY CONSIDERATIONS

In their current stage of development, the empirical studies discussed in the past chapters provide little in the way of definitive policy conclusions. However, they collectively provide considerable support for the hypothesis that regulation has had significant adverse side effects on drug innovation. There would therefore be sizable potential benefits to be gained from improving regulatory performance.

This chapter considers a number of possible policy options for obtaining these benefits. Essentially the discussion is organized into two parts. First, I will examine policy measures that would operate more or less within the existing regulatory framework. Second, more fundamental changes will be considered. The emphasis throughout will be on the way various policy measures can be expected to influence individual or organizational incentives rather than on technical issues.

Organizational Structure and Accountability

Given the existing structure of the drug regulatory process, FDA officials do not have much incentive to be concerned about possible negative impacts of regulation on innovation. First, the regulatory mandate is drawn in very narrow terms—to protect consumers against unsafe or ineffective drugs. There is no corresponding mandate dealing with drug innovation or, in particular, with the need for improved medical therapy.

As I previously noted, the reward structure confronting the FDA regulator is strongly skewed toward the encouragement of risk-averse behavior. The FDA official stands to bear heavy personal costs if there is a bad outcome from the approval of a new drug, but he receives little of the benefits of a good outcome. Moreover, the costs of delay in new drug approvals are borne entirely by external parties.

In recent years, the signals emanating from the external environment have tended to reinforce the incentives toward risk-averse behavior by FDA officials. These signals include, among others, congressional investigative hearings on new drug approvals. FDA Commissioner Schmidt has emphasized the problems these external pressures create for the maintenance of a balanced and rational decision-making structure. He notes:

> For example, in all of FDA's history, I am unable to find a single instance where a Congressional committee investigated the *failure* of FDA to approve a new drug. But, the times when hearings have been held to criticize our approval of new drugs have been so frequent that we aren't able to count them . . . The message of FDA staff could not be clearer. Whenever a controversy over a new drug is resolved by its approval, the Agency and the individuals involved likely will be investigated. Whenever such a drug is disapproved, no inquiry will be made. The Congressional pressure for our *negative* action on new drug applications is, therefore, intense. And it seems to be increasing, as everyone is becoming a self-acclaimed expert on carcinogenesis and drug testing.[1]

In the face of uncertainty about the properties of a new drug, the regulatory official has strong incentives to err on the side of caution and delay. In a world where these properties could be ascertained quickly or where incentive distortions have little cost, this kind of incentive structure would not be cause for concern. However, in the real world, it can produce heavy costs in delays and decreases in drug innovation as well as increases in the cost of research and development and wasted research resources.

The essence of the incentive problem is that the adverse impact of regulation on innovation is generally "external" to the existing regulatory decision-making process. Some means is needed to internalize this impact. One first step for doing so could be to broaden the FDA's existing mandate. In particular,

---

[1] Alexander Schmidt, "The FDA Today: Critics, Congress and Consumerism," speech delivered on October 29, 1974, before the National Press Club, Washington, D.C.

the agency could be given a role in the positive encouragement of new drug development as an incentive for focusing its attention on the effects of regulation on innovation. In addition, various mechanisms could be constructed for ensuring institutional accountability in the area of innovation. A few possible measures along these lines are outlined below.

First, it has been proposed elsewhere that the FDA, jointly with the Department of Commerce, undertake semi-annual reviews of research and development activity and progress on new medicines.[2] The review process also might contain an evaluation of foreign new-product introductions by an external panel of medical experts not chosen by the FDA. Given the fact that new drugs are now generally introduced abroad well before they are introduced in the United States, a valuable stock of information accumulates from foreign usage. This stock is not now systematically used. A formal review of these data, including evaluations of therapeutic benefits and risks, would seem to offer a number of advantages. From the standpoint of regulatory incentives, it would help speed regulatory procedures for new foreign drugs evaluated positively by this group of medical experts.

The FDA might also be required to include in its annual reports a specific evaluation of its regulatory policies on the rate of drug innovation. To date, most analyses of this question have been performed by academic critics. In many ways, the FDA has better data than its critics for studying this question. Moreover, the fact that the FDA would have to undertake and publish such an annual evaluation might encourage the body to take a balanced perspective in the regulatory decision process.

In addition, Dr. Carl Djerassi, one of the developers of oral contraceptives, has proposed that the FDA be required to file a detailed "research impact" statement whenever it issues new regulatory procedures.[3] Such a statement would serve the function of focusing FDA attention on possible adverse effects on innovation.

Diffusion of Decision-making Authority

Another set of policy measures for encouraging a more balanced incentive structure involves greater decentralization of the regu-

[2] The President's Science Advisory Committee, *Report of the Panel on Chemicals and Health,* NSF 73-500 (Washington, D.C.: National Science Foundation, 1973), p. 22.

[3] Carl Djerassi, "Research Impact Statements," *Science,* vol. 181 (July 13, 1973), p. 115.

latory decision-making process. Sir Derrick Dunlop, in his analysis of the U.S. and U.K. regulatory systems, views the greater reliance on professional scientific advisers in the United Kingdom as a major advantage.[4] Professional advisers, whose careers and reputations are firmly established outside the regulatory process, are in his opinion much less prone to a conservative bias in their decisions on new drug introductions than are government bureaucrats.

In recent years, the FDA has formed scientific advisory committees in its different therapeutic categories. Furthermore, it has indicated its intention to promote institutional rather than individual decision making.[5] From the standpoint of regulatory incentives, these moves can be viewed as positive. Of course, their ultimate effect on regulatory incentives depends on the way they are implemented by the FDA.

One further measure along these lines would be the development of some kind of an appeals process on FDA regulatory decisions. In common with most other regulatory agencies established in the United States, the FDA allows for no appeal of an adverse decision short of formal suit in the judicial system. In many other countries, however, there are provisions for such appeals. For example, in the United Kingdom, applicants can appeal an adverse decision of the Licensing Committee to the Medicine Commission, a fourteen-member body composed of scientists, physicians, veterinarians, and representatives of the pharmaceutical industry.[6] A similar kind of appeals procedure might be considered in the United States as an additional check on the regulatory decision-making power.

Pre-Marketing or Post-Marketing Surveillance

The current U.S. regulatory system concentrates regulatory efforts in the pre-marketing evaluation and control of new drugs. Post-marketing surveillance and feedback are somewhat piecemeal in nature and subject to significant lags in response. While drug firms are required to file periodic reports documenting adverse reactions, the companies rely on the voluntary cooperation of

---

[4] Dunlop, "British System of Drug Regulation," pp. 234-237.

[5] See, for example, the Statement of Commissioner Schmidt in Senate, Subcommittee on Health of the Committee on Labor and Public Welfare, *Hearings Amending Public Health Service Act/Food Drug and Cosmetic Act* (Washington, D.C.: U.S. Government Printing Office, 1974), p. 3071.

[6] Dunlop, "British System of Drug Regulation," p. 235.

physicians to obtain this information. There are obvious incentive problems here. Physicians have strong competing demands on their time; moreover, they may avoid reporting adverse reactions because of possible malpractice implications. Hence, this information sometimes goes unreported or else becomes available only with considerable delay. Furthermore, no attempt is made by regulatory officials to collect systematic data on a new drug's beneficial properties.

Regulation in the current system therefore has a bipolar nature. Before approval, drugs are restricted to small patient populations under highly controlled experimental conditions. After drug approval, usage often increases by several orders of magnitude with minimal regulatory surveillance. Under such circumstances, it is not surprising that regulatory officials tend to err on the side of conservatism in new drug approvals. At the same time, despite excessive pre-approval conservatism, many of the adverse side effects of drugs, especially those that are either rare or longer-term in nature, can realistically be discovered only after a drug has been consumed by large patient populations.

An alternative approach to the current "all or nothing" system of new drug approvals would be a gradual monitored release of new drugs.[7] Under such a system, initial usage of drugs would be allowed much earlier than at present but would be restricted to physicians and institutions with special training and resources to monitor the effects of the drugs. These physicians and institutions would be required to maintain close surveillance on patient usage of new drugs and to compile extensive data on their benefits and risks. These data would be tabulated and analyzed by the FDA before the drugs were granted final approval for general use.

A system of gradual monitored release of new drugs offers a number of potential advantages over the current system. First, given the more extensive surveillance and feedback in the first stages of drug release, the FDA would have less incentive than at present to delay introduction of new drugs. Second, a larger body of information would become available to evaluate both the benefits and risks of new drugs before they were approved for general use. This information in summary form would also be useful to physicians as guides to prescription.

---

[7] For further discussion of this concept, see J. Cooper, ed., *The Quality of Advice* (Washington, D.C.: Interdisciplinary Communication Associates, 1974) and Wardell and Lasagna, *Regulation and Drug Development*, pp. 147-148.

The FDA has granted some important drugs (for example, L-Dopa) early release for marketing on the condition that manufacturers monitor and report their effects on a given number of patients. There are thus some precedents in the direction of the gradual monitored release approach suggested above, although to date these precedents have been quite limited in scope. The Kennedy-Javits and Rogers bills currently before Congress both contain provisions concerning the conditional release of new drugs.[8] Hence some important legislative changes in this area could be instituted in the near future.

In light of the potential advantages outlined above, it would seem desirable to develop (and experiment further with) the gradual-monitored-release concept of new drug introduction. It should also be emphasized, however, that this kind of regulatory procedure would only improve matters if it were properly used by the FDA. Unless the incentive is present to reduce pre-marketing hurdles at the same time post-marketing hurdles are increased, then the gradual-monitored-release approach would undoubtedly increase rather than reduce regulatory delays. This possibility is important to bear in mind as new legislation in this area is formulated and considered.

More Fundamental Changes

So far we have not questioned the idea that a centralized regulatory agency should have ultimate control over which drugs can be sold. However, this proposition has been challenged by some academic scholars who advocate greater reliance on market forces as the best means of improving performance in the ethical drug industry.[9]

In Chapter I, it was suggested that the basic rationale for government intervention in ethical drugs has centered on information imperfections. In particular, it was noted that private incentives may be insufficient to generate an adequate stock of knowledge on a new drug's harmful side effects. Furthermore, the information disseminated to physicians by private drug firms may have a self-serving bias. If these propositions are accepted, one could argue logically that the proper role of government in these

---

[8] The Kennedy-Javits bill was introduced on November 20, 1975, to the 93d Congress (S. 2697). The current version of the Rogers bill was introduced on June 9, 1976 (H.R. 14289).

[9] This point of view is presented in several of the papers and discussions in Landau, *Regulating New Drugs*.

circumstances is to subsidize the information process. Alternatively, the government could impose testing standards on drug firms to accomplish the same objective. It does not logically follow from this, however, that the government must also control which drugs can be sold by drug firms or prescribed by physicians.

One might argue that centralized regulatory controls over drug availability are the most effective means of dealing with information imperfections in this situation, but this is not an obvious proposition on a priori grounds. Moreover, one must also take into account the negative side effects or costs produced by a centralized approach.

In addition to subsidizing information, another method the government has for influencing private decisions short of centralized controls is the tort law. The sanctions of the tort law can be used as a deterrent to particular behavior on the part of drug firms or practicing physicians. In the language of economists, the tort law serves the function of internalizing external costs so as to make them an integral part of the decision-making process.

There may be some significant advantages associated with a decentralized approach. Instead of the provision of direct controls, the role of government would be to ensure that adequate and accurate information be available to market participants and that effective deterrents exist against undesirable outcomes. The final decision on the supply and use of drugs would be placed in the hands of private drug firms and practicing physicians. This placement would provide for a more sensitive choice mechanism than now exists—one in which a single binding "yes" or "no" decision would not be required. Moreover, the rewards from a good outcome and penalties from a bad one would not be as asymmetrically distributed as they are under the current regulatory system. Thus, it is likely that there could be a better balancing of benefits and risks than there is under a collective bureaucratic approach.

In practice, the tort law system as it is currently constituted in the United States is somewhat cumbersome and possesses a number of imperfections. These include potential large differences among the parties involved both in legal resources and in the financial stake in the outcome. In the specific case under consideration here there is also a considerable asymmetry in information between producers and users of drugs.

If a shift toward a more decentralized approach to the regulation of ethical drugs were seriously contemplated, some changes in the current tort law system would be required. While this is not the place to discuss this question in any detail, we may note that it would probably be necessary for the government to take a more active role than it now takes in post-market surveillance and collection of information on adverse drug reactions and benefits.[10] In addition, serious consideration might be given to the government's imposing a schedule of contingent liability charges on drug firms before new drugs are marketed, in order to increase the effectiveness of the tort law in its deterrence of adverse outcomes.

The current trend in the United States is for more rather than fewer centralized regulatory controls over product safety standards. While the drug industry occupies a unique position, actual and potential regulation of product safety in almost all industries has increased dramatically in recent years. Congress has created the Consumer Product Safety Commission, empowered to establish mandatory standards and regulate labeling for any class of products the agency finds to be unsafe. In addition, other product classes are now being subjected to pre-market clearance procedures similar to those existing for drugs. The Environmental Protection Agency has recently instituted such a regulatory review procedure for new pesticides, and the FDA has announced its intention to do so for medical aids and devices.

There is thus a clear tendency toward more direct and centralized regulatory controls over product safety in a number of industries. In principle, however, this is not the only approach available for protecting consumers against unsafe or ineffective products. Past experiences with ethical drugs demonstrate that direct controls can impose significant costs to consumers, as well as providing benefits. In light of this, consideration of and experimentation with other regulatory approaches for accomplishing the same objectives would seem to be warranted. In particular, attention to policies that attempt to remedy information imperfections within the basic framework of a decentralized market mechanism could yield high dividends.

---

[10] See, for example, the discussion of this question by Guido Calabresi in Landau, *Regulating New Drugs*, pp. 53-60.